JOE FRISCO

JOE FRISCO

**Comic, Jazz Dancer,
and Railbird**

Ed Lowry with Charlie Foy
Edited by Paul M. Levitt

With a Foreword by Bing Crosby

SOUTHERN ILLINOIS UNIVERSITY PRESS
Carbondale and Edwardsville

Copyright © 1999 by Paul Michael Levitt
All rights reserved
Printed in the United States of America

02 01 00 99   4 3 2 1

Library of Congress Cataloging-in-Publication Data
    Lowry, Ed, 1896–1983.
        Joe Frisco : comic, jazz dancer, and railbird / Ed Lowry with Charlie Foy ; edited by Paul M. Levitt ; with a foreword by Bing Crosby.
        p. cm.
    Includes bibliographical references and index.
    1. Frisco, Joe, d. 1958. 2. Comedians—United States—Biography.
I. Foy, Charlie, 1889–1984. II. Levitt, Paul M. III. Title.
PN2287.F69L68 1999   98-34721
792.7'028'092—dc21   CIP
[b]

ISBN 0-8093-2240-4 (cloth : alk. paper)
ISBN 0-8093-2241-2 (pbk. : alk. paper)

The paper used in this publication meets the minimum requirements of American National Standard for Information Sciences—Permanence of Paper for Printed Library Materials, ANSI Z39.48-1984. ♾

To the memory of Ed and Florrie

CONTENTS

	Foreword *Bing Crosby*	ix
	Preface	xi
	Editor's Acknowledgments	xiii
	Editor's Introduction	xvii
1.	Johnny Newcomer	1
2.	No Excuses in Show Business	3
3.	J-J-Joe Frisco	8
4.	That Kid from Dubuque	12
5.	Her Name Was Loretta	16
6.	Bojangles	24
7.	Jazz via New Orleans	28
8.	Goodbye, Poppa	31
9.	"Oh, Loretta, How Could You?"	37
10.	Rasputin	42
11.	My Broadway	46
12.	This Gorilla Was a Killer	61
13.	Charlie's "Sucker" Club	70
14.	The Joker Is Wild	83
15.	Pass the "Milltowns," Please	95
16.	"Hya Doc, Who Do Ya Like?"	100
	People and Places: A Glossary	109
	"Loretta, How Could You?"	
	An Essay on Chronology *Roberta C. Martin*	133
	Selected Bibliography	149
	Index	151

FOREWORD

Seems like any time people in show business get together for a few drinks, or a dinner, or any other occasion, it always winds up as a storytelling bee about Joe Frisco. Many and varied are the stories one is likely to hear, but they're all funny.

Of course, Joe's delivery—with the stammer—makes a story funnier than when you see it in print, and he had one of the real "dead pans" of all time, which really helped the delivery, too. In appearance he was very neat, always well groomed. Looked more like a bookkeeper, or a librarian, than a comedian—that is, until he opened his mouth and said something.

I know of no combination better qualified to tell the story of Joe Frisco than Charlie Foy and Ed Lowry. Charlie worked with him a lot and lived with him. They were real pals. Ed, a veteran entertainer himself, has a great power of recall. He digs back to the early days of Frisco. He brings Joe back to life in a show business few present-day performers were privileged to know.

I can recall, many years ago, when I was on the radio, once in a while we used Joe Frisco as a guest star, but then a period came along—maybe a year and a half or two years—when for some reason or other we didn't use him. We had other people booked, I guess, and had no spot for him.

One day, he accosted me on the street with his usual greeting, "Hi, Rob." (It seems he called everybody Rob.) I asked him if he caught my show the night before.

He said, "Y-Y-Yes, I c-c-caught it."

"What did you think of it?" I asked.

"Y-Y-You n-n-needed me," was his response.

I guess we'll always need fellas like Joe Frisco, fellas who can lighten up any day with an appropriate crack. He was the master of this.

—Bing Crosby

PREFACE

Joe Frisco never kept a scrapbook. There are few records of names, places, or dates concerning his strange and colorful career. Long before he died, he became a legend to his fellow performers. Yet seldom do any of us agree on where or when Joe first said what to whom. This book, based on the loving memories of Charlie Foy, tries to recapture the Joe Frisco we knew.

Dear Charlie Foy,

It's been many months since we put our heads together and decided to write a book.

Your abundant contribution of Joe Frisco stories made my writing chores a joy. I, too, spent half a century as an entertainer during the same years. We frequented the same places and rubbed elbows with the same people. In fact, Joe and I also had the same agent.

Personality-wise we were direct opposites, yet at times I got so carried away by memories that I found myself switching hats with Frisco—and I look lousy in a bowler.

Don't vouch for the authenticity of everything I put down on paper. Our memories often play tricks on us. Nevertheless, now that I have done the route in my memory for the second time I feel like I have lived two lives. Would you believe, I got just as big a bang out of it the second time around? If our readers are expecting literary skill, this saga will be disappointing. It is not their dish. If they like show business they should bear with us and they will find that we say it the way we play it.

There's our cue, Charlie. Hope we're a hit.
Everybody on stage.
CURTAIN

—Ed Lowry

EDITOR'S ACKNOWLEDGMENTS

In editing this book and identifying its cast of characters, I have had the generous support of a wonderful audience. In the upper circle: Morton Bryer, sales development manager of *Variety*, for offering helpful suggestions and for making available to me archival material; Edythe Handman Colby, retired vaudevillian and former sister-in-law to Florrie Lowry, for outlining the family relationships; Barbara Fidelman, nurse, for checking public records and contacting people in Las Vegas; Warren Garfield, filmmaker, for calling and writing libraries; Howard Kerr, professor of English and Dean of Honors, University of Illinois at Chicago, for solving the mystery of "Rasputin"; Sandra Levitt, actress, for retrieving valuable information in Los Angeles; Scot and Erica Levitt, for lodging me with loving care while I worked at the library of the University of California, Los Angeles (UCLA); Pat Muckle, University of Colorado Writing Program staff and instructor, for tracking down northern California references; Al Palmer, retired locksmith and storyteller *par excellence,* for sharing his incomparable memories of vaudeville; Hedra Peterman, librarian, the Free Library of Philadelphia, for introducing me to the theatre collection at her library; the Research Department of the New-York Historical Society, for making every effort to identify the elusive Fenn Generaux; the staff of the Billy Rose Theatre Collection, New York Public Library at Lincoln Center, for assisting unfailingly and courteously; the staff of the Willard Public Library, Local History Department, Battle Creek, Michigan, for answering my questions with thoroughness and promptness; Robert Steiner, novelist and former professor of English, University of Colorado, for telling me whom to contact in Las Vegas; Jessica Travis of the Historic New Orleans Collection, New Orleans, for radiating professionalism and an eagerness to help; Frank Wright, curator of education, Nevada State Museum and Historical Society, for clarifying some obscure references to people in Las Vegas; and Wayne Larsen, for copy editing the manuscript with scrupulous care.

In the dress circle: Regina Ahram, Interlibrary Loan Office, Norlin Library, University of Colorado, for finding Chicago addresses in old telephone books; Geraldine Duclow, head, Theatre Collection, the Free Library of Philadelphia, for describing the different vaudeville companies and houses; Skip Hamilton, English literature bibliographer, University of Colorado Library, for recommending invaluable reference books and sources; Bruce Boyd Raeburn, curator, Hogan Jazz Archive, Howard-Tilton Memorial Library, Tulane University, for discovering the roots of the Dixieland Five and for sharing material on Joe Frisco in New Orleans; and Doris Jean Waren, librarian, Keeneland Library (Keeneland Association, Lexington Kentucky), for illuminating racehorses and horse races.

In the stalls: Cynthia Coutts, then a Ph.D. candidate in medieval history (UCLA), for verifying names, dates, and addresses in the Los Angeles area; Bruce F. Kawin, professor of English and film studies, University of Colorado, for directing me to important books about film and for lending me works from his own private collection; Richard A. Lanham, professor emeritus of English (UCLA), for allowing me access to the UCLA library system through the services of his graduate assistant; Andrea J. Levitt, entertainment attorney, for locating birth dates of Hollywood actors, checking addresses of theatres, and providing legal advice; Mary G. Marsella, research assistant, for doggedly and amiably pursuing names and places in Chicago; the Rosenfelds—Ben, Jean, and Howard—for identifying addresses and people in Los Angeles and for bestowing other, innumerable favors; and James Simmons, editorial director, Southern Illinois University Press, for believing in the manuscript and bringing it to print.

In the box seats: Laurel Hilton Heywood, former student, for schlepping into Chicago more than once to try to find, in old newspapers, forgotten people and places; Nancy D. Mann, editor and colleague, for providing incomparable editorial advice and assistance; the University of Colorado Foundation for giving me indispensable financial assistance; and Roberta C. Martin, assistant professor of English, East Carolina University, for contributing her valuable "Essay on Chronology," which explores the anecdotal structure of this book.

And in the front row seats: Jane Goldstein, director of communica-

EDITOR'S ACKNOWLEDGMENTS

tions, Santa Anita Park, for identifying every horse and horse race mentioned in the book, for introducing me to the racing world, and for answering all my questions expeditiously and graciously; Elissa S. Guralnick, professor of English, University of Colorado, and my coauthor on numerous books, for spending countless hours on my behalf in New York libraries and for exhibiting the same elegance and thoroughness in her research as she does in her writing.

EDITOR'S INTRODUCTION

Although no longer familiar as a show-business figure, Joe Frisco in his day was so famous for his jazz dance that F. Scott Fitzgerald mentions him when describing one of Gatsby's parties: "Suddenly one of these gypsies in trembling opal seizes a cocktail out of the air, dumps it down for courage and moving her hands like Frisco dances out alone on the canvas platform" (chap. 3). Famous also for his wit, Joe was a notable stand-up comedian for twenty-five years and always a favorite with *Variety* and Walter Winchell's gossip column. In the 1920s, he played the major vaudeville houses, and in the 1930s, the top restaurant clubs, hobnobbing with virtually everyone in the entertainment world. In the 1940s, he moved to Hollywood, commanded a top salary for a few movies, haunted the racetrack, and made Charlie Foy's supper club the place to go. Earl Wilson, in *Let 'Em Eat Cheesecake* (1949), describes attending Joe Frisco performances to hear his *bons mots* and alludes to changing tastes in comedy when he says: "Joe is almost unknown to today's 'younger generation,' but to show-business sitter-arounders, Joe, with his stutter and his derby, is the best of the 'table comedians.' He's the master of the 'rapier retort,' which is different from the 'flip quip.' The rapier retort, of course, is an answer to somebody's remark, while the flip quip is something that can be tossed off without any previous extended colloquy" (p. 44). Joe's type of retort humor, much admired by earlier audiences attuned to verbal wit, had by the mid-1950s fallen out of favor, replaced by sanitized and sentimental repartee.

After Joe's death in 1958, the failure of the popular press and theatre historians to pay Joe his due led Ed Lowry, as he suggests in the preface, to correct this oversight by turning to his friend Charlie Foy, who had for several years shared an apartment with Joe. Charlie owned one of the first supper clubs in southern California, the Charlie Foy Supper Club, located at

15463 Ventura Boulevard, Sherman Oaks, in the San Fernando Valley; in the late 1940s and the 1950s, Joe topped the bill there. The two men lived in an apartment over the club, where Charlie was privy to Joe Frisco's jokes and personal reflections.

The name Foy, to those familiar with vaudeville, recalls "Eddie Foy and the Seven Little Foys," a father, five sons, and two daughters who performed from 1913 until 1923 in a family act of comic sketches and songs. (In a typical skit, one of Eddie Foy's daughters would ask him to bring home a doll. He would inquire what sort, and she would blurt out, "Mama says you know all about dolls.") Charlie Foy, the second oldest child of Eddie Foy and the ballerina Madeline Moranda, appeared not only on stage but also in films. During the middle and late 1930s in particular, he acted in a number of Hollywood films, usually in the role of a small-time gangster. His screen credits include *Down the Stretch* (1927), *Fugitive in the Sky* (1936), *Here Comes Carter* (1936), *Hot Money* (1936), *Adventurous Blonde* (1937), *Dance, Charlie, Dance* (1937), *Melody for Two* (1937), *Midnight Court* (1937), and *Penrod and His Twin Brother* (1938). He also at this time made a number of Vitaphone shorts for Warner Brothers, among them *Blackwell's Island* (1939), *Conspiracy* (1939), *Hell's Kitchen* (1939), *Mutiny in the Big House* (1939), and *The Wagons Roll at Night* (1941).

During World War II, Charlie served at the Hal Roach Studio making informational, documentary, and propagandistic films for the Armed Forces special services film unit. With the conclusion of the war, he briefly supported himself as a talent agent; but finding the work uncongenial, he returned to the stage, performing at his own supper club, which he began in 1941 and operated for a time at two locations in the San Fernando Valley. In 1955, he narrated the feature film about his family, *The Seven Little Foys*.

Charlie Foy died in 1984 at age eighty-six.

Ed Lowry died at almost the same age, eighty-seven. Born in 1896, he entered show business at fourteen as a hoofer, having learned his first dance steps from a mail-order course. He subsequently expanded his routine with singing, eccentric dancing, and comedy. His first success came as part of a husband and wife team. He and his first wife, Irene "Teddy" Prince, left Gus Edwards's *School Days*, where they had met, and launched their own career in Chicago.

EDITOR'S INTRODUCTION

Eventually Teddy withdrew and Ed went solo, having advanced from the obscurity of the second spot (number two act) on vaudeville shows to the premiere position of next to last. In the waning days of vaudeville, he traveled to England as a tourist and found himself offered a stint at the London Palladium. Unaware of the rule requiring a work permit, he performed at the Palladium until the authorities ushered him off to police headquarters, where Nora Bayes extricated him from his difficulty.

Upon returning to the United States, he became part of that strange, early hybrid entertainment in which theatres offered audiences both movies and variety shows on the same bill. Engaged by the Skouras brothers as a master of ceremonies, he became during the 1930s one of the most prominent and sought-after emcees on the film and vaudeville circuit, hosting per day as many as five variety shows between films. In this capacity, he helped develop such stars as Betty Grable, Dick Powell, Louis Prima, and Ginger Rogers.

During World War II and then the Korean War, he worked in Los Angeles for the United Services Organization (USO) Camp Shows, organizing the one-night shows brought to servicemen stationed at home and abroad. Ed not only recruited the specialty people—jugglers, hoofers, acrobats, comics, mimics, and novelty acts—but also arranged transportation and accompanied some of the touring troupes in the capacity of manager. As part of the largest circuit of entertainment the world had ever known (a survey revealed that on a single day, five hundred separate shows had been presented under USO auspices in various military installations around the world), Ed gained invaluable administrative experience, which he subsequently put to good use in buying and operating a hotel in Beverly Hills and speculating in real estate in North Hollywood.

Two years after Teddy's death in 1967, Ed married Florrie, with whom he lived until his death in 1983. It is from Florrie that I received this manuscript.

Florrie Lowry, born Evelyn Florence Mills in 1897, began dancing classes at twelve and made her professional debut a year later, singing and dancing at movie theatres in and around Philadelphia. Her mother, who traveled with her, gave her the stage name of Florrie Le Vere. At sixteen, under her mother's guidance, Florrie moved to New York to advance her career. By then her act, entitled "Celebrities," presented impressions of well-known stage stars of the period. In New York, she met her future husband, Lou Handman, a pianist, songwriter, vaudeville performer, and song plugger for Irving Berlin. In 1925, Florrie and Lou teamed up as Le Vere and Handman and took their act on the road. A year later in New York they married.

Their act played the leading theatres of the day, including the top vaudeville theatre in the country, the Palace. They traveled throughout the United States and, in 1928, to Australia and New Zealand. Florrie remained active on the stage until Lou took sick in 1955, at which time she retired, caring for Lou until his death a year later. In 1965, she moved to California, where in 1969 she met and married Ed Lowry. They knew each other from the days when Ed had appeared on the stage with his wife, Teddy Prince. Florrie died in 1990 at age ninety-three.

How Florrie came to give me the manuscript about Frisco is a story in itself. Florrie rented a lovely apartment in Beverly Hills, on North Palm Drive, near Beverly and Doheny. Although infirm, she lived alone, assisted by a weekly visit from a nurse. My mother, who regularly called on Florrie, invited me to join her. I did so eagerly, having heard for years that she was a rich source of theatre lore. When my mother and I arrived at her door, we had to wait several minutes before she could answer our ring and disengage the lock. Once in the apartment, we sat in the living room on a long couch, while Florrie, dressed in a robe and slippers, curled up in a club chair, explaining that she spent a good part of each day resting in bed. For the first half hour, my mother and Florrie exchanged pleasantries and reminisced about the songwriter Lou Handman, Florrie's first husband and our cousin; hence the connection with Florrie. Then she began talking about Ed Lowry. During the course of her recollections, she mentioned Ed's love of writing and his habit of keeping "books" in which he recorded all his skits and jokes. When I asked if those books might still be about, she gestured toward a narrow closet a few feet away and said that as far as she could recall, they had been stored in a carton on the shelf. But because she stood under five feet and the shelf towered above her, she had not opened the carton in years and thus could not vouch for its contents. Observing that vaudevillians and their brand of humor had gone out of fashion, she directed me to take whatever I liked.

At the top of the closet, wedged between the shelf and the ceiling, rested one large, unmarked carton. Although six feet two, I had to stand on a chair to remove it. Inside I found four neatly arranged notebooks: (1) jokes, (2) skits, (3) Ed Lowry's autobiography, entitled "Dear Audience," and (4) a manuscript with the cryptic title "Heart Aches and Horse Laffs," followed by the curious inscription: "by Ed Lowry as told by Charlie Foy." What, I wondered, had Charlie Foy told Ed Lowry? Not until I opened the manuscript and read a copy of Bing Crosby's letter (the original seems to have disappeared) did I realize that the title referred to the comedian Joe Frisco. I carted off the manuscripts and returned with them to Boulder. A year or two passed; the news of Florrie's death reminded me that my primary sources were passing with the old vaudevillians. I set to work sorting through all the material, cataloguing the jokes and skits, and reinforcing my knowledge of American vaudeville by contacting people who had seen the shows or worked in them and by reading numerous histories of the period and the performers. Perhaps such study might explain why Joe Frisco, of *Gatsby* fame, was no longer remembered.

I noticed immediately that most vaudevillian humor had been satiric and that much of the satire would now be regarded as racist, sexist, or culturally biased. In general, the vaudeville comedians trafficked in jokes about blacks and Jews, about the "dizziness" and prodigality of women, and about the allegedly national traits of Dutch (Germans), Irish, and Italians, among others. But as the 1950s were themselves none too free of racial and ethnic humor and as, in any event, Joe Frisco's jokes rarely exploited stereotypes, he could not have lost favor because he (or vaudeville in general) was politically incorrect.

Rather, Joe Frisco's fall from favor resulted from changing tastes in humor owing to expanding technology. Television created a revolution in entertainment—and not merely by complementing sound with the visual. That would have made TV a natural medium for vaudeville, as indeed it was in its earliest days. Nor was the move from a public space to a domestic one the sum of the revolution. Had that been the case, vaudeville would merely have moved from the stage to the living room—and remained there. But as television, with its multisensory appeal, began eclipsing radio, it was simultaneously spreading beyond its origins in the large cities of the Northeast, which favored satire, to the countryside, which favored sentimental comedy. This shift, argues Arthur Frank Wertheim (1983), killed vaudeville.

A case in point, according to Wertheim, is Milton Berle's *Texaco Star Theatre,* which featured frenetic vaudeville humor. From 1948 to 1952, when the show was televised in cities, it was hugely popular. But from 1952 to 1954, as coaxial cable and new stations spread television to rural America, Berle's raucous comedy no longer kept him at the top of the charts. The *Texaco Star Theatre* lost its preeminence to *I Love Lucy;* coruscating wit and *ad hominem* ripostes gave way to soft gags. For the most part, comedians now told safe stories, their jokes no more pointed than Groucho's famous misplaced modifier about shooting an elephant in his pajamas.

In an era of sentimental humor, the only place left for Joe Frisco to dance and exchange rapier retorts was in nightclubs. But nightclubs in turn declined in popularity and number as people stayed home to watch TV. Joe's world was shrinking. Although he tried his hand at movies, he and his directors agreed that Joe Frisco, stand-up comedian, was made for the stage, not for film. The only other place where Joe might have prospered was, of course, the page, which has always been hospitable to his kind of verbal wit. This, I suspect, is why Ed Lowry undertook to write a book about Joe Frisco: because he felt that print offered a way to preserve Joe's comic genius.

Joe Frisco: Comic, Jazz Dancer, and Railbird is a rare piece of Americana, a collector's item, though it can by no stretch of the imagination be called a biography. According to the eminent historian Sir Ronald Syme (1971), biography "furnishes a framework and a chronological sequence"; and the chronology, of course, is expected to be accurate. As Ed Lowry indirectly acknowledges in his preface, this manuscript does not meet even that elementary test. *Joe Frisco: Comic, Jazz Dancer, and Railbird* proceeds not chronologically but anecdotally, unfolding like a series of articulated jokes held together, as Roberta Martin points out in her concluding essay, by the recurrent themes of Joe's sweetheart, Loretta McDermott, and Joe's mother. Whether Joe was in Chicago or Detroit on a certain date probably cannot be determined with any accuracy from this manuscript. Lowry and Foy were not particularly interested in the man who was born Louis Joseph and brought up in Dubuque. What they wrote was not a scholarly biography but a memoir—a kind of document that ranks with letters and diaries among those "place[s] of beginnings" that the writer of a full-scale biography must "revisit," as Ira Nadel (1993, p. 15) observes, in order to see the subject through the eyes of his contemporaries.

EDITOR'S INTRODUCTION

Because Lowry and Foy were contemporaries of Frisco and because they wrote about him vividly, their memoir, even if unreliable about places and dates, is nonetheless a rich resource for biographers, cultural historians, and theatre critics. Lowry and Foy describe Joe Frisco's world, with its hotels, theatres, restaurants, clubs, racetracks, and, not least, its famous people—Flo Ziegfeld, W. C. Fields, Walter Winchell, George Jessel, Bing Crosby (who contributed the foreword to this book), even William Randolph Hearst. Lowry's and Foy's invaluable contribution is to revive a lost era in American theatre by bringing again to life the myth of Joe Frisco, tragic clown.

My own contribution has been to revise Ed Lowry's text so that Joe's luminous wit stands unfettered by misadventures in style, punctuation, spelling, and paragraphing. To enhance the book's value for biographers and historians and the general public, I have also contributed a glossary that succinctly identifies (where possible) the many people and places that populate the text. If the reader takes from this book as much pleasure as I took from editing it, then my purpose—as well as Charlie Foy's and Ed Lowry's—will surely have been realized: to entertain the public with the heartaches and horse laughs of one of the great American comics, Joe Frisco, as remembered by two fellow entertainers.

JOE FRISCO

1

Johnny Newcomer

Though many thousands of actors and entertainers have faded from memory, one comedian always comes to mind whenever and wherever show folk meet. As soon as a group of entertainers start reminiscing, this man is quoted and often imitated. His memory survives merely by word of mouth. He never made it big in the movies or TV, so he is not seen in replays or revivals. His deathlessness is strictly the result of mouth-to-mouth resuscitation.

To account for the durable charisma of this man, one must conclude that there is little in life more impressive than humor. He certainly didn't have the charm of Chevalier, the voice of Sinatra, or the pathetic kisser of Chaplin. His face was devoid of expression. It was a face that never lit up. When he popped a humorous line at you, you were never prepared for it. It hit like an explosion. The guy loved to talk but couldn't finish a three-word sentence without stuttering. When you first heard his name, you rightly surmised he was the godson of a freight train or a California city.

Christened Louis Wilson Joseph, he was forced to give up his identity on his first theatrical assignment, when he was called to the office of Nate Feinberg, a small-time agent. The interview was brief. Feinberg did all the talking.

"Don't tell me how much you want; I'll tell you what you are gonna get. And about that name they pinned on you . . . Louis Joseph; it's ridiculous. Sounds like two first names. Big people are known by their last names, like Caruso or Chaplin. An attraction with two first names? That's for my competitor," he chided.

His stenographer impatiently inquired, "What name shall I put on the contract, sir?"

Gazing out the window, Feinberg focused on the railroad tracks across from his office. He saw a string of passing freight cars on "The Frisco Lines." "That's it!" he shouted gleefully. "Frisco—F-R-I-S-C-O—make it Joe, Joe Frisco. That sounds good."

And so, with that brief ceremony, Louis Joseph was laid to rest and Joe Frisco was born. The rebirth took place around 1912 in Chicago, where Joe entered the theatrical arena as a "hoofer." It was a long time before Joe got famous enough to be called by his last name. In fact, during those early days he was seldom called at all. He became known as a dressing room comedian, an offstage clown. But he could find no onstage outlet for his humor. The cheap, small-time theatres and cafes were not geared for stand-up comedians. The entertainment had to be physical and visual, so Joe pounded away on his quest for fame as a dancer.

Eventually an enterprising New York agent saw him perform in a Chicago cafe and was impressed by his unique style. Thanks to that chance encounter, Joe Frisco, after ten years of struggle for recognition, invaded Broadway.

2

No Excuses in Show Business

Unimpressive, looking like a tourist, Joe was sitting in front of a huge, highly polished desk. He had just completed reading a "bit part" that he hoped to play in a skit.

The great Ziegfeld sat back in his overstuffed, shiny leather chair, amazed but not amused. "Holy Christ," he exploded. "Do you always stutter like that?"

"No sir," replied Frisco, "only when I t-t-talk."

Harry Fitzgerald, veteran theatrical agent, said hurriedly, "Mr. Ziegfeld, after your audience sees this boy dance, they will readily excuse the impediment in his speech."

"Excuses, Mr. Fitzgerald, excuses! There are no excuses in show business. Florenz Ziegfeld did not make his reputation on excuses. My stock in trade has been laughter and beauty. I seek the most beautiful women in the world and hire the finest writers to supply the laughter. This boy is not beautiful and he is not funny."

Gene Buck, who had helped produce and write most of Ziegfeld's epics, cut in.

"Flo, this particular scene is played in front of the ticket office of a railroad station. People are standing in line, impatiently waiting to buy their tickets and rush off to their trains. This boy's natural stutter will make the scene. He holds up the line trying to make the agent understand. He wants a t-t-ticket for P-P-Pittsburgh, which he finally gets after much delay. Now two more people get taken care of. Next, it's Walter Catlett's turn. He too, buys a ticket for Pittsburgh. Without looking up, Walter rushes toward the gate and collides with our stuttering friend.

'Excuse my haste,' says Catlett, 'I'm catching the six o'clock train for Pittsburgh.'

'Ya better hurry,' says the little guy. 'I just m-m-missed it!'"

Ziggy laughed heartily and said, "I'll buy that."

Now Frisco spoke up. "Mr. Ziegfeld, I need an advance of one hundred dollars. I hope you'll b-b-buy that!"

Harry Fitzgerald all but leaped out of his chair, "Joe," he shouted, "have you blown your top? What in the world would prompt you to ask for an advance on your salary before you're even hired?"

"It's my teeth," explained Joe. "G-g-gotta get my d-d-dentures fixed. Bad enough to stutter, want me to c-c-click too?"

That line tickled Ziegfeld, and he threw two fifty-dollar bills on the desk.

Well, if Joe Frisco was calling on a dentist, this dentist had his office at the racetrack. Within a half hour Joe Frisco was on a Long Island train, on his way to Belmont Park. He arrived in time for the first race, and to quote Joe, the only luck he had that day was—he got a ride home.

Two weeks later Florenz Ziegfeld proved that he could glorify beautiful women and also, by his magic, supply enough levitation to elevate an unknown, small-time hoofer to stardom. Backed by twenty-four beautiful girls attired in leotards, short jackets, and bowler hats and puffing on big "prop" cigars, Joe Frisco made his Broadway debut. To the tune of "The Darktown Strutters' Ball," he, his derby hat, and the king-sized cigar made theatrical history. He puffed on the corona, shuffled his feet, rolled his hips, and contorted his body just as he had always done in the honky-tonks. On this night, after he twirled his bowler, flipped it back on his head, and tilted it rakishly over his eye, he put his hands in his pants pockets and started shuffling toward the exit. The applause sounded like a thunderclap.

Was this dancing? We had seen the grace of Fred Astaire, Pat Rooney's waltz clog was a joy to watch, Bill Robinson tapped his way into our hearts; but this—this weird concoction—was this dancing?

Broadway first-nighters are always on the alert for new faces. They like old jokes and old jokers, but show them a new face with a fresh approach and the response is instantaneous. On this night the new face belonged to Joe Frisco. The new approach introduced the first jazz dance ever seen on Broadway.

When shows such as these open in New York, it's customary for the players to stay up all night and wait for the morning papers to hit the street. Corks pop and elbows bend until the dailies arrive. Then the players gather in groups and eagerly read the critics' reviews.

It was on an occasion such as this that Joe paraphrased the late Will Rogers by saying, "All I know is what they read to me from the papers." What they read to Joe that night was beautiful. The critics raved over this strange character. In the lingo of the street, he walked away with the show. Immediately he became an important part of the Broadway scene. The Joe Frisco dance became a craze. It swept the country; Joe became one of the most imitated entertainers of his day.

Ziegfeld's party on that opening night was a posh affair.

Grant Clarke, who wrote most of the lyrics for Ziegfeld, as well as many top pop songs, was Frisco's close friend. They were joyously clicking their glasses together when composer Irving Berlin stepped up. Berlin raised his glass in tribute to Frisco and in his thin, soft-spoken voice extended his congratulations. As the great little guy walked away, Joe cracked, "What a sweet man, b-b-but you have to hug him to hear him."

Comedienne Fanny Brice, who was within earshot, laughed. Fanny was leading a distinguished-looking gentleman by the hand. "Joe Frisco," she shouted, "come here; I want you to meet Mr. William Randolph Hearst." The famous newspaper publisher smiled amiably, then in a fatherly tone said, "My boy, I enjoyed your performance. I admire creative people. Work hard and some day you will be a big success." Shaking his hand firmly, Joe looked right into the face of the old gent and stuttered, "D-D-Ditto, Mr. Hearst."

A few steps behind came the glamorous Miss Davies, who said, "Mr. Frisco, you were a smash tonight." Then offering him her hand, she said modestly, "I'm Marion Davies."

"Oh," responded Joe, "you're the b-b-broad that goes around with that guy that s-s-sells newspapers." Marion Davies laughed until she cried. As a result of the smart-aleck remark, Joe and Marion became lifelong friends. Seldom did she give a party to which Joe wasn't invited.

Grant Clarke now nudged Joe. "Here comes that damn Harry Richman. Stinker, I'd like to put Pluto water in his martini."

Along Tin Pan Alley, Richman was called Mr. Payola. Every song he sang became a success. The music publishers were willing to pay any price to have their songs introduced by the inimitable Richman. Joe received the compliments of this dapper, well-groomed guy—and drooled. "Mr. Richman," he said, "all this c-c-coming from you is more satisfying than a d-d-dish of apple pie à la mode. There's only one thing could make me happier."

"What's that?" asked Harry.

"That suit you're wearing," responded Joe. "When you g-g-get tired of it, I'm in room 314 at the Somerset."

Hearing Joe eat humble pie infuriated Grant Clarke. He was the writer of the hit song "Am I Blue," and he made the mistake of trying to tell Harry Richman how to sing it. The enmity between the two men became so fierce that one night they came to blows on the dance floor of the Club Richman. The newspapers blew up the account of the fracas out of all proportion. Actually, neither could hit hard enough to crush a cream puff.

Grant cringed at the friendly repartee between Richman and Frisco. "Joe," he said, "don't fall for this guy's arrogance. If it weren't for my songs, he'd be wearing a suit made of burlap."

"On him it would look good," cracked Joe, but his humor missed fire.

"Ingrate," shouted Richman, "if I hadn't sung your songs and got them off the ground, you'd be working as a busboy."

During this confrontation, Harry was gesticulating wildly, and the ashes from his cigarette landed in Grant's martini.

"Did you see that?" Clarke screamed. "He deliberately dropped his cigarette ashes in my drink."

"It's good he doesn't chew tobacco," consoled Joe.

The insults grew more pungent and the two gladiators were about to lock horns when Gene Buck made his appearance. "What the hell is going on here?" he demanded.

Frisco volunteered the reply.

"I think Grant is g-g-gonna take Richman again."

The next day in his column, Walter Winchell gave that crack prominence by printing it in bold type. Since Mr. Hearst was his boss, Winchell in his gossip column never quoted Frisco's little gem about Marion Davies and her boyfriend who sells newspapers. But Winchell did include this amusing observation: "Joe Frisco, who got the most enthusiastic notices from the critics, was the only member of the cast who refrained from reading the complimentary passages over and over, out loud. A rare combination—talent and modesty."

Modesty? Hmph! Winchell missed the boat on that one. Joe Frisco didn't know how to read. Completely illiterate, he was unable to write home to his mother because he couldn't spell *Dubuque.*

3

J-J-Joe Frisco

Broadway at this time boasted another producer and star maker similar to Ziegfeld: Gus Edwards, a wizard at picking children with theatrical potential. His *School Days* was a veritable incubator for talent, giving birth to Cantor, Jessel, Groucho Marx, Jack Pearl, Mae Murray, Hildegarde, and Eleanor Powell, to name just a few.

Gus Edwards chafed at the unprecedented success of Joe Frisco. He claimed that every other youngster who now walked into his studio to audition carried a derby hat and a prop cigar. It has often been said, for example, that it was Joe Frisco's popularity that started Jessel smoking cigars at fourteen; and for years George wouldn't be found without his bowler hat, not even in bed.

Loretta, Joe's first partner and sweetheart, was among the thousands of teenagers who auditioned for a part in one of Edwards's productions. Gus had a way of convincing a doting mother to wait in the outer office while he had a little chat in his inner sanctum with the daughter. Whether Loretta gave Joe a sordid description of what went on during her "chats" with Gus we'll never know. We do know, however, that the very mention of Edwards's name used to rile Joe.

One night Frisco was seated at the bar of a popular Forty-seventh Street restaurant and Gus Edwards came through the door. Frisco stood up on top of his chair and shouted loudly:

"Hide your children, everyone; here c-c-comes Gus Edwards."

This gag was still good for a laugh twenty years later when sixteen-year-old Lois Andrews became the bride of George Jessel. Immediately Jessel replaced Gus Edwards as the butt of the joke. It was surefire again, and all the comedians jumped on it.

The number of people who copied Joe attests to the durability of his humor. When jobs got scarce, many of his imitators worked while he was laid off. With a shrug of the shoulders and a flick of his cigar, he'd comment, "Some of these guys who imitate me do me b-b-better than I d-d-do myself—and cheaper too!"

While out of work, Joe always found an eager audience in the hotel lobby, at the racetrack, or in the Hollywood Brown Derby. Being broke never bothered him. He was America's guest. Although a compulsive horseplayer, he never wanted for anything. His life took on a pattern. Someone always picked up the dinner check, bought the drinks, and responded to fifty- and hundred-dollar touches.

The one place where Joe had to come up with cash was at the track, at the pari-mutuel window. Here he was a master at getting nothing for something. He described the clerk as a pickpocket who let you use your own hands. One of these so-called pickpockets described the action the day the world-renowned Busher ran her first stakes race at Santa Anita.

Movie tycoon Louis B. Mayer, who had paid over a hundred thousand dollars for the horse, bet five dollars across the board. Highly regarded attorney Neil S. McCarthy, the man who purchased the horse in Ireland for Mayer, bet ten dollars on his "baby." Fred Astaire bet ten to win and ten to place; and following Fred, Cary Grant casually walked to the window to make his customary wager—two dollars. Meanwhile, there was a scene at another window. Chico Marx was buying a ticket, and Al Ritz was anxiously pushing Marx. Climbing up the backs of both of them, fearful the window would close and shut him out before he got his bet in, was Joe Frisco. This, you guessed it, was the hundred-dollar window.

As a rule, all Joe had in his pocket was a hole. Yet he frequented the finest restaurants, where his presence was always considered a plus. In Dave Chasen's swank restaurant, however, he had the welcome mat pulled from under him. Half a dozen of Dave's celebrity patrons had bought Joe drinks. Dave noticed that Frisco was staggering badly as he worked his way to Sinatra's table. Frank, too, noticed that Joe was well in his cups. He embraced Frisco but, instead of buying him a drink, folded up a hundred-dollar bill, put it into Joe's hand, and said, "Pal, you're loaded, go outside and grab yourself a bundle of fresh air." Joe mumbled his thanks and moved toward the entrance. He held the door open, inhaled a couple of times, then muttered, "Fresh air—hm, it's poison." He turned around and walked right back into the establishment. Chasen, fearing he couldn't handle Joe, called for a squad car. Two friendly officers quietly took Joe outside. When he sat down in the police car, he apparently thought he was in a cab. He leaned forward and said, "Driver, take me to the Foy S-S-Supper Club." Then he passed out.

Some time after three A.M., Charlie Foy arrived at the police station. Thanks to Sheriff Biscailuz, arrangements were made to release Joe to Charlie. Joe had had five hours of sleep, and the hundred-dollar bill was still in his pocket. Foy thanked the officer profusely, said, "Let's go, Joe," and started to leave the station. When he reached the front door, Frisco wasn't with him. He retraced his steps and found Joe at the desk talking to the officer in charge.

"What now, Joe; what do you want?" inquired Charlie.

"I'm making a reservation for t-t-tomorrow night," was the reply.

Joe loved to pin stories on Crosby. At Foy's Club he once announced, "Ladies and gentlemen, greet the most popular man in the world, Bing Crosby." Bing took a bow to tumultuous applause.

"Congratulations, Bing," shouted Foy. Then turning to Joe, he asked: "How do you know he's the most popular man in the world?"

"It's true," persisted Joe. "It was in a magazine. There was a poll, and B-B-Bing won by four hundred thousand votes."

"Who ran second?" questioned Foy.

"I don't know," Frisco retorted, "but the P-P-Pope came in third and p-p-paid $2.80 to show."

Occasionally Bing took Joe to dinner. Once it was at the fashionable Perino's restaurant, which featured chafing dishes, meat served on flaming swords, and blazing desserts. Joe, who was wearing a lightweight suit, watched with great interest the flaming food being served. The headwaiter finally arrived and asked if they wished a table.

"No," replied Joe, "we just came in to g-g-get warm."

Shortly after the Japanese bombed Pearl Harbor, Charlie Foy proudly walked into the Brown Derby wearing his army uniform. He was frail and looked his forty years. Crosby spotted him and said, "Here comes Charlie Foy." Joe peered through the dimly lit room. "You're crazy," he told Bing, "that's a boy scout."

"No, no," Crosby insisted, "it's Charlie in a uniform. What the hell do they want with Foy in the army?"

Said Joe, "The b-b-bookmakers wanna make the Japanese the favorites."

These gags circulated like chain letters and continued to do so until one-liners, except in Saint Louis, lost their cachet. Fifteen years after Joe died, Bob Hope and Bing Crosby, on a network television show, swapped Frisco stories and got "yocks."

Professional storytellers usually prepare and set up an audience for what they are about to hear. For instance, the hackneyed line, "A funny thing happened to me on the way to the theatre tonight," is used to make you think you're about to hear a new story. At an actor's club, like the Friars or the Lambs, if you preface your story by crediting it to Joe Frisco, it's a pretty surefire guarantee that the yarn won't bomb.

4

That Kid from Dubuque

Joe was born in Milan, Illinois. When he was five the family moved to a farm on the outskirts of Dubuque, Iowa. Poppa Joseph bought and sold livestock. On the farm is where the young Joe started to follow the horses—but with a shovel, not a *Racing Form*.

Mrs. Joseph was warm and gregarious. For hours at a time she would enthrall her young son with stories of her theatricals. Always the boy gave an eager ear to her ecstatic memories. She became incandescent when she relived her short career in English pantomime. By the time he was seven, young Louis had been taught to do a Lancashire clog. Momma's joyous tales of the past were quite a contrast to the drab surroundings on the farm. Much of his mother's love for the stage clearly rubbed off on the son and planted the seed that eventually bore fruit.

At every opportunity Louis ducked away from the farm, so he could pal around with kids from the town. The other boys called him Joe, short for Joseph.

One day, an exciting attraction played the local opera house: Eddie Foy in *Over the River*. Every night the customers lined up four deep. This show inflamed Joe's imagination. He, too, wanted to perform. Recalling his mother's stories about "buskers"—English street entertainers who did their stunts on the sidewalk—Joe, assisted by two other teenagers, formed a trio and made his debut as a street performer.

One boy's contribution consisted of slapping his hands together in rhythm. The other boy played a Jew's harp, or at least so he claimed. To this orchestral background, Joe did his Lancashire clog dance. At the conclusion, a few coins fell to the ground. Encouraged, Joe now sprinkled some sand on the sidewalk and announced, "Ladies and gentlemen, I will now show you a soft shoe sand dance." When he had finished, a few more coins hit the pavement. The three kids then passed the hats around and to their delight discovered that the crowds were very liberal. After three nights of these performances Joe was so pleased he felt that in comparison to himself John D. Rockefeller was a bum. He bought his mom a full pound box of chocolate creams and temporarily stashed away the balance of the loot. Walking home that night, Joe decided that he would find a partner who played harmonica. The music would sound better, he reasoned, and there would be only two ways to split the money.

Several days later, flushed with excitement, he rushed into the house. "Momma, momma, look!" Proudly showing her a brand new pair of shoes, he explained, "See these metal discs? The shoemaker attached them for me. Now when I dance, these two pieces of metal will hit together and my shoes will jingle." Never had he been so intensely happy and proud as at this moment. The boy, however, hadn't noticed his father sitting in a rocker next to the stove. The old gent got out of his chair, put his glass of beer on the table, and walked toward Joe. He demanded:

"How much did you pay for those shoes?"

"Six d-d-dollars," stammered Joe.

"Six dollars!" thundered the father. "Idiot, do you know how much bread that would buy?"

He then grabbed for the shoes, but Joe screamed, "No—please, p-p-please don't t-t-take 'em from me," and he hung on tenaciously.

At first the father couldn't make the boy release his hold. Joe clung with every ounce of strength he could muster. It was as if his very life depended on these shoes—these beautiful shoes, his most valued possession. Suddenly Poppa Joseph was holding the shoes under his arm. He headed for the potbellied stove, lifted the lid, and threw the shoes into the fire. Joe stood there sobbing. He was ashen white and wild with anger. Impulsively, he bent forward, lowered his head, rushed for his father, and butted him in the stomach. Poppa Joseph let out a yell and fell over backward. In a panic, Joe bounded for the door and ran down the road with the speed of a gazelle. Years later, describing the scene, he said, "I b-b-broke the track record. I made the first six furlongs in 1:09 flat!"

It was merely Poppa's feelings that were hurt. "Oh," he moaned, "wait until I get my hands on that goddamned little monster." The mother intuitively knew he never would.

Joe thought he was heading for Chicago, but somehow he hopped a freight train that ended up in Milwaukee. A job as a stable boy for a brewing company kept him in food, but as the days and weeks wore on it grew monotonous. His fondness for horses and his willingness to work impressed the stable boss. After a friendly chat, the man advised Joe to apply at the front office for a better job. A pedantic old fuddy-duddy in charge of personnel handed Joe an employment application form. Joe just sat and stared at the form.

"What's wrong?" inquired the sourpussed gentleman. "Can't you write?"

"I c-c-can't read, either," admitted Joe.

"Well," piped the clerk sarcastically, "my friend is the dean out at the university. Would you like to try out for his debating team?"

"I did," snapped Joe. "I was t-t-too t-t-tall."

Early the next day Joe got a hitch on a brewery truck, and late that night he arrived in Chicago. On the following day, he started a new career as a Western Union messenger boy. An interviewer once asked Frisco how he first came to show business. When he replied, "by Western Union," this was more factual than funny.

As Western Union was located downtown in Chicago's Loop, most of the messages Joe delivered were to theatres, theatrical agents, and actors. In those days Chicago was jumping with show business. In every neighborhood there were little theatres playing vaudeville. Even the nickelodeons on State Street that were showing two-reel flickers featured spotlight singers. The Majestic, the big-time vaudeville theatre, was the flagship of the Orpheum circuit.

There was one vaudeville factory known as the Great Northern Hippodrome. Here they had sixteen acts: four shows a day on two shifts. Eight acts worked from eleven A.M. until four P.M. The other shift performed from four to eleven P.M. If you got into the theatre at half past two, you saw sixteen acts for twenty-five cents. Here Joe got his first peek backstage. He was delivering a telegram to Freddie James. The stage doorman had wandered off for a moment, and Joe wandered in. Oh, how he enjoyed that first smell of greasepaint and a look behind the scenes. He tiptoed downstage and from the wings he watched Freddie James. The card on the easel read, "The world's greatest juggler." He was really the world's worst, but the audience howled as he bungled every trick.

Freddie James was a man we all knew later as Fred Allen. In his later life, Joe Frisco got many a bum tip at the racetrack, but he never forgot the fifty-cent tip he got from Fred Allen.

Joe not only got lucky at the Great Northern Theatre, he did even better at the Great Northern Hotel. He delivered a telegram addressed to the room clerk, who, before signing for the wire, ripped open the envelope, read the message, and let out a whoop loud enough to wake up the dead. He had a winning ticket in the Irish Sweepstakes.

"Son," said the clerk when he got back down to earth, "what's the biggest tip you ever got?"

Proudly, Joe told him, "Got a half d-d-dollar from an actor yesterday."

"Well, brace yourself, kid," said the excited clerk. "You are getting a twenty-dollar tip right now."

With twenty big ones in his pocket, Joe decided to send half to his mother. But how? He still couldn't spell *Dubuque*. Mrs. Dunn, the head telegraph operator, convinced Joe that the safest way to send money was by wire. Off went the ten dollars, and Joe was happier than the guy who won the Sweepstakes. Now Joe's friend Mrs. Dunn shamed Joe into repeating the spelling of *Dubuque*. When he finally had memorized "D-D-D-D U B-B-B U-QUE," he laughed and said, "Now with m-m-my luck, mom will m-m-move to Cedar Rapids."

5

Her Name Was Loretta

On Randolph Street, Kitty DeLacey had a rehearsal hall and dance studio. One day Joe went there to deliver a telegram to Mrs. DeLacey. At the moment of his arrival, she was in the midst of doing a dance routine with a line of ten girls. Joe sat on a bench and, while waiting, was highly entertained. At the conclusion of the routine, Kitty came forward, eagerly reached for the telegram, and ripped it open. She was having a running feud with her husband via Western Union. The contents of this wire made her fume.

"Girls," she shouted, "keep working." Then turning to Joe, she directed, "You, young man, wait. I wish to send a reply."

Joe again sat on the bench. He was pleased with himself; he was wishing that writing the reply would take all day. It was like watching a three-ring circus. One girl was doing back bends; another, high kicks and splits; others were just limbering up or doing back kicks while hanging on to a wall rail. Over in a corner one kid was pounding out a time step. Joe couldn't see her face, but he admired her shape and beautiful legs.

Kitty DeLacey returned. She handed Joe the written message, turned on her heel, slapped her hands, and then commanded, "Okay, girls—PLACES!"

Joe left—but returned frequently. Soon he noticed that the face of the little tap dancer was as attractive as her body and legs. Her name was Loretta McDermott. "A living doll," Joe thought. By the fourth visit, Joe was smitten. He waited downstairs, and when rehearsal was over, he tailed after the little tapster. He had a pretty good line by now, and it took only a few more visits to convince Loretta that he had dancing feet and that he knew all the booking agents.

"We'll p-p-put together a few routines, get some good-looking photos taken, show 'em to the agents, and then you j-j-just leave the rest to me."

Loretta had mixed feelings about "leaving the rest to him." On the one hand, her mother had made a deal with Kitty DeLacey. In return for instruction, Loretta was committed to dance with the line of girls for a minimal fee whenever the troupe played local jobs. On the other hand, she was itching to escape from this disciplinarian. Kitty was strict. Loretta pouted every time she was corrected and sassed back constantly. "Joe might be a good out," she thought. Instinctively, however, she played hard to get. "After all," she told Joe, "I'm a pro. For six weeks this summer I was in Gus Edwards's *Song Revue."*

She neglected to say that her complete performance was to sit on a piano while Mr. Edwards played. For three minutes, she and another little Kewpie doll clad in nightcaps and pajamas sat starry-eyed while Gus sang to them of soda fountains and ice cream mountains. Though Joe was a Western Union boy again, he felt that he, too, was a pro. Hadn't he worked three nights for Nate Feinberg? If he hadn't stuttered on his lines he'd still be with Nate.

In no time, they started rehearsing together and worked unceasingly. Actually, Joe drove too hard. Loretta craved less work and more attention. "Gee, Joe," she complained, "you don't give a girl much 'house,' do ya? Ya know I could have signed with Gus Edwards for three years . . . but hot dog, he's too much!"

Joe ignored the gab and kept right on dancing.

Loretta rambled on. "Talk about bosses chasing stenographers around a desk! Oh, daddy—he starts off by picking you up and sitting you on his desk—ha, then try to get away."

This chatter Joe remembered forever. Was it true? He never knew; but he could never like Gus Edwards afterward.

A strenuous week of rehearsal and planning, and the team of Loretta McDermott and Joe Frisco was ready to travel. After a short ride on the El, somewhere on the West Side they found their first date. The place was called the Sans Souci and could hardly have been called a theatre; actually it was a spaghetti house. It had a regular stage, however, with a roll-up curtain, a row of footlights, and an orchestra consisting of piano and drums. For fifty cents, the customers got a full-course spaghetti dinner with wine and four acts of vaudeville. Starting at five P.M., the Sans Souci staged a show every hour. Between shows the actors were welcome to all the spaghetti they could eat. At two A.M., the place finally shut down. They might not have closed then if Loretta hadn't eaten them out of spaghetti.

The day after their performance at the Sans Souci, they had an interview at the Buchanon, Irving Agency. Mr. Buchanon, a disarming little gent, wore a goatee and looked like a doctor. He booked them for that same night. Since they were new, he reasoned, this was actually a tryout or a showing, so "Let's not call it a salary; we'll just say expenses, say, er, four dollars?" They took it!

When they arrived at the Verdi Theatre, they learned that Mr. Buchanon not only booked the theatre and managed it but also owned it.

Mr. B. liked their act. After the show he came backstage and offered them bookings for Friday, Saturday, and Sunday at the Victoria Theatre. Twenty-five bucks for the three days! Subsequently, they played some small theatres for Mr. Irving. He was even more generous. He paid them five-fifty a night.

Quickly they began to learn the ropes. Some of these little theatres would book in five or six acts, knowing they were going to retain only three. After the show was over, the acts would sit in their dressing rooms, dreading the possible knock on the door. The knocker was generally the manager. Accompanied by a burly stagehand, he'd hand you your photos and growl, "Pack up, you're closed!"

There was one little castle in Chicago called Schindler's. Mr. Schindler didn't knock on your door. He would walk right down the aisle in full view of the audience, hold up his hand like a traffic cop, and shout, "Dot's enuff, you're shut!"

One Saturday night, they were playing a little arena called the Palace. Loretta was onstage acting real cute with a song called "My Sweetie Went Away." She was clad in a pair of kid's rompers. Suddenly, one of the monkeys got loose, wandered onstage, looked Loretta over, and decided to make "patty-cake" on her bare legs. Joe was in the wings changing his costume. He had just taken off the trousers that he wore in his Bowery number. When he saw what was happening to Loretta, naturally he got excited. It was probably the only time in his entire life that Joe displayed gallantry.

Still holding his trousers in his hand, he rushed out on the stage and stood there in his drawers. The crowd howled. He tried to shoo off the monkey, but the little monster then decided to make "patty-cake" on his bare legs. Our hero stood there petrified. Now there were more monkeyshines by the little devil. He turned and leaped up on Joe—arms around the neck and legs around the waist, all set for a piggyback ride. Just then the trainer came running onstage.

Joe looked at him pitifully and said, "Mister, your monkey is loose."

"Yeah, I see," said the trainer. He took the monkey by the hand, and as the little rascal made his exit, he looked back at Joe and slipped him a big juicy raspberry.

As Lew Lehr of Fox Movietone News used to say, "Monkeys is the cwaziest people."

One day Joe got lucky. He found an agent who had not seen their act. The man was stuck. He needed a team to leave immediately for New Orleans. He'd booked a small place down there called the Pink Poodle. "This is a real fine spot," he said impressively. He was pleased with Loretta's appearance on the photos but said it was imperative that Joe wear a tuxedo.

"I've got a tux," fibbed Joe.

"When a man is stuck he can't be choosy," the agent admitted. Within an hour, arrangements were made. He handed Joe two railroad tickets and a twenty-dollar advance in salary. His last instructions: "Don't forget the tuxedo."

In spite of Joe's speech impediment he could put on a very plaintive appeal. His friend Andy Clark had a beautiful tuxedo. Andy was a headwaiter but temporarily unemployed. His suit fit Joe perfectly, and minutes later, the tuxedo traveled.

This trip to New Orleans was a new experience for Loretta. It was her first time away from home without her mother. The mother was worried and had good cause to be. Her daughter was a natural-born flirt; she knew just when and how to turn on the peepers. On the train, as soon as Loretta sat down, she snuggled over and cuddled up to Joe. When she set her sights on a guy, you could always put your money on her. What Loretta wanted, Loretta got, and it was generally a one-way street. If a guy got a crush on her and the feeling wasn't mutual, she was tougher to handle than Resista, the little gal in vaudeville that no one was able to lift off the ground. Joe was a pushover. This was his first romance. Immediately, he became the world's most satisfied citizen.

Stuttering Joe made a six-syllable word out of *l-l-love,* but apparently this didn't add to his appeal; Loretta thought he was as romantic as the wet toast under a poached egg. He knew how to express his great love for his mother, but it never occurred to him to share some of this tenderness with the little gal who had him hooked. Right from the beginning, Joe took Loretta for granted. She didn't seem to mind; she loved his sense of humor. Together they learned to laugh at adversity, and this made for a good partnership, at least to start with. When they stepped off the train in New Orleans, they were all atingle. The city was enormously exciting. Bourbon Street was wild, but the Pink Poodle was anything but the class joint the agent had described. It was a honky-tonk.

Loretta and Joe didn't fare very well there. A Chicagoan's version of a Bowery dance done in New Orleans bored the audience. They then went into their soft-shoe dance, which included a little patter. "You know, Joe, when my father was born, he weighed only three pounds." As they danced, Joe asked, "D-D-Did he live?" The Pink Poodle crowd was not amused. Then came their *pièce de resistance,* the finish of their act, a Texas Tommy dance. Five minutes after they left the stage came the knock on the door.

When the manager brusquely pushed the photographs into Joe's hand, the whole world crashed in. They had seen this happen to others, but "G-G-Good God, not us d-d-down here in Louisiana." Joe tried to detain the manager. "Wait a minute, p-p-please," but this guy seemed to enjoy his chore. To rub a little salt in the wound, he turned to Joe and sneered, "Kid, if you're an actor, I'm a watchmaker."

Now Loretta popped up. "A watchmaker, you big bum; I bet you can't even tell time."

Joe was too speechless even to stutter, but Loretta, full of moxie, said, "Let's get out of this joint. I wanna get a look at New Orleans. Let's live it up if it's only for twenty minutes."

They were attracted to a place called the Creole. Out front there was a big sign: "The Dixieland Five." Loretta perked up as soon as she heard the music. Joe was still brooding, "We certainly must have s-s-stunk up the place for that manager to g-g-get so mean."

"Boy, listen to that music; what a band. C'mon, Joe, let's go." To be holding Loretta in his arms was a cure for anything in those days. "What rhythm!" They danced and drank and spent their few remaining bucks carelessly.

Next morning when Joe gave an accounting of their funds, there was no whimpering. "Seventeen cents," Loretta laughed. "Gee, I thought you said we were broke—let's have breakfast."

They each had a cup of coffee and a chocolate-covered doughnut and still had two cents left. "Might need these t-t-two cents for dinner. The p-p-penny machine is loaded with p-p-peanuts!"

After their hearty breakfast, Joe got an inspiration. He took Andy Clark's tuxedo to a pawnshop and came back with seven dollars. He then walked to the Western Union office and sent a telegram to the Hodkins Booking Agency in Oklahoma City. He informed Hodkins that McDermott and Frisco had just closed a successful engagement at the Pink Poodle Cafe and were available for immediate bookings in the vicinity.

Within a few hours, they got back a response—$1.95 collect. "Bookings for the Nemo Theatre in Algiers, Louisiana, for Saturday and Sunday. Salary $18 net and offer for last half of following week at Baton Rouge—four days, $45. Confirm."

The little cigar box known as the Nemo Theatre suited them perfectly. Not only did they become enriched to the tune of eighteen dollars, but their confidence got a needed boost.

With a few dollars in their treasury, they were again lured to the Creole Cafe. The saying "I'd rather dance than eat" was actually true of these two. Now with this music they were in their own world, improvising new steps to this new rhythm.

On their second visit, the other revelers gradually cleared the floor to watch Joe and Loretta. They were getting fancy. He'd swing away from Loretta, do a rhythmic shuffle on his own, then a jivey, bouncy movement that would get him back to his partner. She melted into his arms and followed every move. Even the musicians on the bandstand applauded, and the leader bought them a drink.

Wednesday morning they went to the Pink Poodle in search of mail.

The doorman handed Loretta a telegram. Joe was jubilant: "B-B-Bet it's Hodkins offering more b-b-bookings."

"Oh yeah," countered Loretta, "listen to this—'Just got good job send back tuxedo immediately.' Signed Andy Clark."

That night on their last visit to the Creole they became friends with the Dixieland Five. Each of the boys bought a drink between sessions. Joe and Loretta got stoned and took to the dance floor by themselves. After more applause than they had ever received before, Joe held up his hand. "D-D-Don't applaud, folks," he shouted. "Just throw m-m-money." Darned if they didn't gather in more loot than they had earned for the two days at the Nemo Theatre across the river.

The four days at Baton Rouge were a letdown: poor audience response, no further bookings, and after the engagement, not enough money left to buy two tickets to Chicago.

Loretta weighed only eighty-five pounds and was four feet eleven. "I have an idea," she said. "If you have the nerve to go through with it, I'll travel to Chicago on a half-fare ticket. We'll pretend I'm your baby sister."

The next morning, wearing a child's dress, white socks, baby doll shoes, and a big pink bow in her hair, she coyly clung to Joe's hand as they boarded the train. It was July, but no one else on the train was perspiring like Joe. Loretta lay down with her head in Joe's lap and her feet on the other half of the double seat. Joe spread a newspaper in front of his face and pretended he was reading. He not only couldn't read, he did a lousy job of faking it. The conductor smelled a rat. Each time he walked down the aisle, he lingered by the seat, and Joe got a cold sweat. Finally, he inquired, "Doesn't the little one ever sit up?"

"No," replied Joe, "when she sees a c-c-conductor, she gets t-t-train sick."

At long last, they pulled into Memphis. It was announced that there would be a four-hour layover before departing for Chicago. Loretta reneged on wearing the kid clothes for the four hours in Memphis. In the station, she ducked into the ladies' room and changed to her street clothes. As she emerged in her high-heeled shoes, she bumped smack dab into the conductor. With all the authority of a sheriff or a constable, he grabbed her by the wrist and gave out a big "Ah ha!" Loretta fainted. He then blew a whistle to call the stationmaster—and Joe fainted.

Dramatically, Loretta told her tale of woe. The stationmaster was impressed. When the train pulled out of Memphis, they were on it. It was three A.M. when McDermott and Frisco pulled into Chicago's LaSalle Street station. Weary and hungry, they started walking. When they reached State Street, they set down their suitcases to rest their weary arms. They were attracted by a drunk. He had a bag of doughnuts under his arm and was feeding them to a traffic cop's horse.

"What a lucky animal," said Loretta enviously.

After the horse had devoured and relished about twenty doughnuts, Joe exclaimed, "How in the hell can anyone eat all those doughnuts without asking for a cup of c-c-coffee?"

Bojangles

The next couple of years were toughies for Joe and Loretta. Joe moved into Chicago's Inter-Ocean Hotel at State and Van Buren. Here he got a room with free coffee and doughnuts every morning for three dollars a week. The Inter-Ocean was a typical theatrical rooming house. The small lobby buzzed with troupers. Most of these performers were called "suitcase actors," a label that gave them a definite classification. They were small-timers who carried all their earthly belongings in—and practically did their acts out of—their suitcases.

Joe joined the parade. Almost every night he and Loretta would lug their suitcases up and down the steep steps and ride on the el until they reached their destination. This was usually a little bandbox that they called a theatre. By the profession, these little one-night stands were politely referred to as "dumps." The salary was generally five to eight dollars a night for a team. Not much money but a means to an end—experience. Sometimes, sadly, experience is all you've got left after everything else is gone.

One night at a little soapbox called the Casimir Theatre, way out on Milwaukee Avenue, Grace Van Buren happened to see their act. Her boss, Walter Meakin, booked a small circuit of out-of-town theatres. Two days later, they were playing the Unique Theatre, in Staples, Minnesota. Next came the Bijou Dream in Ashland, Wisconsin, followed by some pips that even Rand McNally hadn't yet discovered. After several months of these real smallies, McDermott and Frisco jumped up several notches. Walter Meakin maneuvered them into a four-week booking on the Butterfield circuit, starting at Battle Creek, Michigan.

Bill Robinson, whose legendary name was Bojangles, was the headliner. The magic of this man's feet fascinated Joe Frisco. No wonder they also referred to Bill as the Chocolate Nijinsky; dancing made him feel joyous, and to Joe that joy was contagious. One morning Bill came to the theatre long before matinee time hoping to find some mail. Joe Frisco was on the dimly lit stage practicing a dance routine. Bojangles stood in the wings and silently watched Joe labor. "Mr. Joe," he said after a while, "Ya know what you're trying to do? You're trying to squeeze six pounds of sugar into a five-pound bag." Eventually Joe got hep to what Bill was trying to say to him. He changed his routine and got twice as much applause for half the effort.

This was Joe's first professional advice. Bill Robinson was a super show-man. During those four weeks, Joe Frisco learned much about dancing and got a liberal education in wowing the crowd. He learned other things as well from Bill. He learned, for instance, never again to be a matchmaker in a pool hall. He also learned why Bill Robinson could run faster backward than most people could run frontward. "Often he got in trouble," said Joe, "and he had to s-s-start running before he had time to t-t-turn around."

Bill shot pool as well as he danced, but away from New York and Chicago it was difficult for a Negro to get a game. The only integration a man like Bill could enjoy in those days was backstage. He could be the headliner at the best theatres but could rarely get accommodations at the best hotels. In Saginaw, Michigan, the only living accommodations Bill could get were just back of the railroad station. There he rented a furnished room with a black family. These were working people who rose at six and retired at nine. Bill got home the first night at ten-thirty. He sat in his dimly gaslit room listening all night to train whistles.

The following afternoon he enlisted Joe's aid not to find him a room but to find him a pool game. Joe got an audience with the proprietor of the town's best pool parlor. The man had seen the show the previous night and was impressed. Bill Robinson, the headliner at the Strand Theatre, issued a challenge that he would play any man in town a fifty-point game of straight pool for fifty dollars. Every pool parlor has its champ, and every town has its share of gamblers. At eleven o'clock that night the pool hall was jammed. Bill Robinson was in his glory, and Joe Frisco was proud. He had made his debut as a promoter and a crusader. Now came another first: he made a five-dollar side bet on his own.

Before the match, Bill put on quite a show. Warming up, he handled the pool cue like a musician would a slide trombone, playing a tune with his cue, directing each ball toward another as he walked around the table in rhythm. The taps just seemed to roll after him. The onlookers were in a gay mood for the contest. The opponent was quiet, tall, sallow complexioned, and as thin as Slim Summerville. Bill played first. He chalked his cue, walked around the table, and bent down so his vision was table high. Finally, instead of going for a safe break, he held up his hand for attention and announced, "I'll play the six ball in this left corner pocket."

The audience was shocked by Robinson's audacity, and Frisco gulped as Bill's cue went into action. The racked balls broke in every direction. The six ball, as though having an independent life all its own, rolled into the left corner pocket.

"Boy, how lucky can you get," cracked one of the spectators. Bill glared at the speaker. He held up the play, reached for his wallet, slapped it on the frame of the pool table, and said nastily, "How would you like to put your money where your big mouth is? I'll do it all over again, just for you; that is, if you got some folding money that says I can't."

The heckler responded with a Bronx cheer and a few obscenities that fortunately were not too audible.

The proprietor stepped forward. "Mr. Robinson, you'll kindly put your wallet away and continue the game. Mr. Frisco assured me this would be a gentleman's match. If we can't retain our dignity, I'll refund the money and call the contest off."

Bill wasn't slapped down too easily. He mumbled some gibberish about his dislike for sore losers. Joe, smelling trouble, moseyed over to Robinson and pleaded with him to be calm and continue his play. Calmly, Mr. Bojangles chalked his cue and proceeded to knock the balls into the pockets, just as if they were hypnotized. When he finally missed, the miss was a heartbreaker, a cliffhanger that just barely hung on the edge of the pocket.

Now it was his opponent's turn. Make no mistake about it, the man was good but not in a class with Bill. He was a real champ, Bill was, but when he got way out in front, instead of being gracious, he became an obnoxious exhibitionist. He started banking shots unnecessarily and, instead of holding his cue in the customary manner, made a few intricate shots while holding the cue behind his back. All this to belittle his opponent.

"Congratulations," said the proprietor, handing Bill the money. "You gave a fine exhibition; thank you, and good night."

Bill ignored the brush-off. The loser congratulated him, but Bill tried to goad the man into a little more action by offering a ten-point handicap on another game. The thin man declined. He admitted he was outclassed.

The five dollars was the first bet Joe ever won. After he collected he tried to persuade Robinson to go home.

"Mr. Joe," said Bill, "you've got a nice room to go home to. I'm a black man; what's waiting for me is a dreary room in a fleabag down by the railroad tracks. You go find Miss Loretta and take her to coffee. Thanks for everything, and I'll see you tomorrow."

Next morning at the theatre, Joe found a very humble Bill Robinson. There was a plaster patch on his chin, and he was holding an ice bag on his head.

"Mr. Joe," he inquired, "would you favor me by taking my shoes to the repair shop? I sure will appreciate it."

He had run down the steep steps of the pool hall so fast that he lost the heels off both his shoes.

The Joe Frisco who returned to Chicago after this tour was a much more seasoned trouper and showman. He now dreamed of combining his act with the Dixieland Five—and he had the determination to make the dream a reality.

"With the New Orleans group backing us with that new rhythm, we'll be an attraction," he persistently told agent Meakin. Meakin believed in Joe, and Fritzel believed in Meakin.

7

Jazz via New Orleans

So it came to pass that Chicago's oldest agent was responsible for Chicago's newest craze—jazz! Joe Frisco, a nonmusician, supplied much of the drive that got this new fad off the ground.

Because Mike Fritzel's Cafe was in the basement, Joe referred to his new showcase as an upholstered sewer. But Joe never had it so good. The first thing Joe did when he got established in his new job was noble. He bought his friend Andy Clark a new tuxedo and convinced Mike Fritzel to give Andy a job as headwaiter.

The act was now billed as "Joe Frisco and the Dixieland Five, assisted by Loretta McDermott." Within four weeks' time, Mike Fritzel's "upholstered sewer" was turning away customers six nights a week. Soon the attraction was in such demand they were doubling, playing in both the cafe and the better neighborhood theatres. This was real labor, but they all loved the extra compensation as well as the sweet taste of success.

At the Kedzie Theatre, Hank Edwards, a singer who also played vibraphones, attracted Loretta. His sound fit in with the Dixieland music perfectly, and his specialty on the vibes would give Joe a breather between numbers. Naive Joe, who couldn't say no to Loretta, hired Hank.

On a weekend holiday, when business at the club was at an all-time peak, Charles Joseph, Joe's elder brother, called from Dubuque. Their father was in a bad way. "The doctor's prognosis after a lengthy consultation was that there was no hope for recovery. Mom would like you to come home."

Joe wasn't moved until his brother explained, "Mom is badly shaken and grief stricken. She's blaming herself for the breach between you and Poppa. She has developed some kind of a guilt complex: in fact, right now

Momma is in an emotional state bordering on hysteria. You must come home, Joe."

"Chuck, I'm—I'm—er gee, c-c-can I call you later?"

"Later may be too late, Joe."

When Joe arrived home, he and his mom clung to one another—and sobbed on each other's shoulder. It was a release for both of them. As he held her in his arms and felt the warmth of her love and devotion, he was almost joyous, in spite of the misery around him. His sister, Mae, brought him up to date about the father. "He has cancer," she explained. "He's been suffering unbearable stomach pains for many months. The drugs and painkillers have become practically ineffective. He is down to skin and bones, but Dr. Burke says he has the heart of a lion."

When Joe and his mother entered the sickroom, Joe was relieved to see that his father was either sleeping or in a coma. The old man's little, shrunken face was scary; it looked like the face of a cadaver. Joe was grateful for the momentary pause that gave him time to generate enough false courage to face his ordeal. His mom's last instructions were, "Joe darling, embrace Poppa and kiss him on the cheek. Give him that little pleasure, please; is that asking too much?"

They sat by the bed and Momma held the little man's hand. He breathed heavily, and after what seemed like forever, he stirred.

Joe was so panicky he froze.

His mother took Joe's hand and placed it on top of his father's. Joe feared he would faint. "Oh God," he thought, "please get me out of this; this is torture."

The stricken man turned his hand and weakly grasped Joe's. It seemed like a drowning man clutching a straw. He tried to look up toward Joe's face, but he couldn't focus properly. Momma spoke up. "Poppa, you know who's here to see you? It's our baby, our baby boy. He came back home to see you." She was sobbing now.

"Hello, D-D-Dad," stuttered Joe. "I'm g-g-glad to see you." That was as far as he got. With what little strength his father had left, he pulled away his hand. He tried to talk but couldn't. There was a rattle in his throat, then a few short gasps, and it was over. Poppa Joseph was dead.

"I'm a murderer," sobbed Joe. "I killed Poppa, it's my fault, I did it." Suddenly Momma fainted. Fortunately, she was still in the chair and almost instantly her daughter, Mae, was on hand with smelling salts. During the confusion, the doorbell rang. The family doctor had arrived at just the right moment.

First, he officially declared Poppa Joseph dead. As he was a country doctor, his little black bag contained just what every member of the family needed. He gave Mother a pill that immediately put her to sleep, and the rest of the family were given sedatives. Curiously, the most hysterical member of the family was Joe—curious, because there never had been any manifestation of affection between the father and son. Instead of being sympathetic toward Joe's speech impediment, his father, as far back as Joe could remember, had ridiculed him. Joe always felt put down in his father's presence. As he grew up, he was called on to perform only the most menial farm jobs. Never, ever, was the old man known to give the frustrated son who needed it most an encouraging tap on the shoulder.

8

Goodbye, Poppa

Several hours after the final curtain, the brothers were sitting on the back steps talking. They were nipping out of a pint bottle of bourbon, which they passed back and forth, while Joe poured out his heart. He retold the ugly story of using his head like a ram to butt his father in the belly. He confessed that he had spent many sleepless nights repenting. And yet, he pointed out to his brother, "With me, Poppa was more like a bully than a parent."

"Mom never forgave him for throwing your shoes in the fire. She thought it was cruel, and it hurt her even more than it did you, but," continued Chuck, "he's gone now, so let's only remember the nice things he did."

"I will if I can think of any," said Joe bitterly.

"Kiddo, you have nothing but contempt for Poppa's memory, so how come you're so goddamn hysterical over his death?"

"My grief is for Momma. My stinking temper has brought her all this misery. I p-p-probably caused his death when I butted him in the s-s-stomach. That was the b-b-beginning."

"You're weird," was the brother's comment. "Tell me, how the hell did you work that out?"

"That bruise in his abdomen. I was to b-b-blame for that. That s-s-started him downhill. I know I caused his death, and Poppa knew it, too."

"Poppa knew you caused his death? Holy Jesus, how do you come to that, now?"

"A few seconds before he died, Mom put my hand in his and said, 'Poppa, here's our baby boy.' He was too weak to blink an eye, but he managed to pull his hand away from mine t-t-to show his contempt for me. He tried to s-s-say something then, but it was too late. I thank G-G-God for that 'cause he would have called me a killer in front of Momma and I'd never be able to live with myself again."

Recognizing that Joe was taking upon himself undeserved guilt, Charlie tricked his brother into accompanying him to the doctor's office. He pretended he was going to request some extra death certificates. But before they left the office, Dr. Burke gave Joe a clinical review, revealing the medical history of the entire case. The father had had a malignant disease, which progressed and became terminal and incurable.

"No bump, bruise, or physical injury," emphasized the doctor, "had any connection whatever with the illness or the demise of the patient."

"I hope you're satisfied," said Charlie, as they walked out of the office. "Now let's go have a drink."

Joe's mind was eased, but he always harbored a little bit of doubt. It certainly changed his whole pattern of life. Never again was Joe Frisco known to lose his temper or indulge in any form of physical violence. His tongue became his weapon.

By coincidence, on the same night that Joe Frisco left Chicago for Dubuque, Hank Edwards, the vibraphone player, took off for Peoria. Hank decided that this would be a good chance to get home to visit his wife and three children.

Now that Loretta learned that Hank was married and had children, she forgot him—for almost a whole day. She was shocked, crushed, and jealous. She had fallen hard for Hank. As the lonely days passed with Joe and Hank both gone, her cravings intensified. She decided Hank was a stinker to go home to his family and leave her alone. She formulated a plan to get a tighter hold on Hank. Joe didn't know it, but he was going to be used.

Deception can sometimes be beautiful. When Joe arrived back in Chicago, the plot he walked into could have come right out of a well-made play. He was overwhelmed by the warm reception and affection he received from Loretta. Never before had she been so demonstrative. Joe was carrying around with him a hurt, and right now Loretta was just what he needed. Loretta, too, was feeling hurt. Unfortunately, Joe wasn't the cure that she needed; but his sincere response to her phony acting pleased her greatly. She would have been the first to admit that it was comforting and consoling to sense that Joe wanted her.

The return of Joe Frisco and the Dixieland Five, assisted by Loretta McDermott and Hank Edwards, turned out to be a gold strike for Mike Fritzel. The club was jammed; the customers were hanging from the chandeliers. Mike Fritzel did everything but push the walls out to seat a record number of patrons. The dance floor, which also served as the stage for the entertainment, was crowded by the addition of at least a dozen extra tables. At each table there were four chairs. The people were practically sitting on one another's laps.

Women in formals and men in dinner suits and some in tails were pushing and crowding each other. Every night was a dressy turnout, but in those days in Chicago, the man wearing a tuxedo could very well have a gat in his pocket and a sawed-off shotgun in his car.

Joe complained that there was no space left for him to do his dance properly. "You've got the dance floor so cluttered I'll b-b-be the first guy in the world to do a d-d-dancing act without moving my feet."

"You're just the guy that can do it," said the boss man.

"Yeah, then I'll talk without m-m-moving my lips and I'll be the first s-s-stuttering ventriloquist."

"All I care about," said Fritzel, "is getting the extra money in the bank to make up for the bundle I lost by your absence last week."

"I cried enough for myself last week," said Joe. "D-D-Don't expect me to cry for you, too."

"Frisco, you better learn the first fundamental of show business, or you'll cry plenty: the show must go on. You don't just up and leave town without a minute's notice."

"I went to my m-m-mother. She needed me."

"The other seven people in your act also needed you. You threw them out of work. The man who hired you needed you as well. He had to refund hundreds of dollars. This show must go on tonight, if you have to dance on a dime."

"I'll d-d-do my best," Joe assured him.

"Good," said Fritzel, "and by the way, if you ever duck out on me again without notice, don't bother coming back."

Bill Robinson, who was considered an all-time great tap dancer, won numerous awards without his feet even being seen. Frequently during a contest, the judges would sit in a basement under the stage and just listen. Bill never sluffed a tap, nor did he ever labor. His grace, ease, and style came right through the sound.

The night that Joe Frisco reopened at Fritzel's the audience went wild with enthusiasm. They repeatedly broke in with applause all through the dance. As with Bill Robinson, his rhythm, his movements, the big cigar, the explosive puffs of smoke, plus the twirling bowler hat and the expressive gyration made his audience forget to look at his feet. There were so many encores that Joe ran out of material. On an impulse, he did a trick his mother had taught him. He whipped out the handkerchief from his top pocket. Two corners became rabbit ears; another corner became the rabbit's tail. He then put the rabbit under his left arm. Two fingers now became the rabbit's mouth, and it ate up the carnation that was in his left lapel. So great was the laughter and applause from this sophisticated audience that he incorporated this playfulness into his subsequent performances.

After the show Joe had much table-hopping to do. He suggested that Loretta return to the hotel instead of waiting for him. Hank Edwards was going right home, and he volunteered to give Loretta a lift. Loretta accepted, and Joe said, "Thanks Hank. Take care of my baby." How could anyone so clever be so dumb?

Mike Fritzel was exuberant. "Nice work," he said to Joe. "This is the biggest crowd we ever had in one night."

"It's good you didn't crowd any more t-t-tables on the dance floor or I'd have had to ph-ph-phone my act in."

Joe booked many jobs that night. He was wanted for a dozen different affairs ranging from an important Italian wedding to a Shrine convention. There was little bickering over price. Joe was hot. One incident, however, marred this beautiful night. A patron invited Joe to have a drink. Joe sat down, not knowing that this man had become obnoxious and belligerent. Violence had to be avoided, so at the same time that Joe joined this man's table, a Mickey Finn was being mixed to use on this guy as a pacifier.

"Bring my friend Joe Frisco a bourbon and water," shouted the loud-mouth, "and bring me the same."

"Coming up," said Andy Clark, who was delighted to have such a fine assist from his friend Joe. He returned almost immediately and set the bourbon in front of Joe and the Mickey in front of the goon. The intended victim had a hunch, so when Joe turned for an instant, he switched the drinks. Joe Frisco drank the Mickey. "That's oil, brother," Joe was moved to say, as he began to pass out.

Business continued to be brisk, and Joe's popularity held up remarkably well. He played extra engagements three and four times a week, sometimes solo and sometimes with the group. Everyone was sharing the success, and everyone was happy.

Several months after the death of the elder Joseph, tragedy again befell the family. Charles was shot in the head. When Joe's mom called, she explained briefly that Charles had taken a job as a bartender. There had been a fight between two drunks; Charles interceded and had been shot for his labors. Mom pleaded with Joe to come home and be with her during these trying times. He tried to beg off. Mike Fritzel's tirade was still fresh in his mind: "The show must go on," and "If you ever leave me again without proper notice, don't bother coming back."

"Mom, darling, it t-t-took me a lot of years to g-g-get where I am. I'm making b-b-big money and I can't just chuck it."

"Joe," she pleaded, "it won't cost you much. Charles had a little insurance, and the veterans will help; and Joe," she continued, "I have four hundred dollars I've saved on the side. Please, son," now she was sobbing, "I need you."

"I'll be there, Momma, and d-d-don't worry about money. We'll get Charley the best doctors no matter what it costs."

As he hung up the phone, he shouted, "The hell with Mike Fritzel. I've been a hell of a b-b-bust as a son. Mom saved four hundred dollars in all these years. I made more than that last week. Shame on me."

In spite of Joe's illiteracy and speech impediment, he had an abundance of chutzpah. At a most ungodly hour, he got on the telephone and succeeded in getting through to Dr. Max Thorek.

Dr. Thorek was the founder of the American Hospital in Chicago. He once was credited with saving the life of Eva Tanguay. She was so grateful for and respectful of his outstanding ability as a physician and surgeon that she pledged to help set up a foundation for him. With her aid and with help from other popular stars of the day, his dream was realized.

The doctor was famous for being a friend to the profession. He established that fact quickly with Joe. In a few hours, Joe Frisco and an eminent brain specialist were en route to Dubuque. But it wasn't to be. They arrived too late; Charles was dead. Sister Mae and her husband attended to all the funeral arrangements, while Joe stayed close to the side of his mother. The truth is that he felt like a stranger, having been away from home for so many years. He also felt guilty. Though he tried to be comforting, he was awkward, remembering when the roles were reversed and Momma was the mountain of strength, reassuring and always anxious to help him. She seemed just as worried about him now as before. She feared he wasn't eating properly. Wasn't he ever going to consider coming back home and settling down?

"Have you got a girlfriend, Joe?" she inquired.

"Yes, Momma, my girlfriend works in my act. We've been friends a long time. I'm really stuck on her," he confessed.

"What's the matter; does she think she's too good for you? Why aren't you gonna get married?"

"I n-n-never asked her, Momma."

"Well, you should. A person your age shouldn't be running around the country alone. Have another piece of steak; you eat like a bird."

"Thanks, Mom, but I'm full. You're really a g-g-good cook." She patted him on the cheek. "You're still a good boy, Joe, but being alone is not good for you. You get lonesome and get into mischief like poor Charles did. If Charles had married he wouldn't have been working in a saloon. Find yourself a wife, my boy. God didn't mean for anyone to be alone."

Joe was smothered in this kind of conversation for a full week. His love for his mother reached the point of being pathological, but he was ever so relieved when he left for Chicago. While sitting on the train he meditated, realizing how far removed he was from the scene he was leaving. Dubuque was a different world entirely. Momma had become a little old woman, God bless her. "She treated me like I was Baby Snooks." He smiled at her philosophy: "Get married and you won't get in trouble." Most of the guys he knew got in trouble by getting married. Yet there seemed to be so much more to life when he was around Loretta. "Maybe Mom's right at that," he mused; Momma was always right. "God, am I confused."

9

"Oh, Loretta, How Could You?"

The train roared into the station. Joe was the first one on the platform. He wanted Loretta to be standing at the passenger gate waiting for him, but she wasn't.

Before he got in the cab, he stopped off in the drugstore and bought a beautiful bottle of toilet water and had it gift-wrapped. This was a first for Joe Frisco.

At the hotel, he found that Loretta had changed her room. She was in 217 now.

"How come?" inquired Joe.

"You'll have to ask her that," replied the clerk.

Joe knocked on the door, but there was no reply. He knocked again, loudly. After a pause, Loretta asked, "Who's there?"

"It's me, honey," shouted Joe eagerly.

"Er—a—Joe? Er gee, I-I-I didn't expect you so soon. I'm not decent at the moment, J-J-Joe. Hang on a minute."

When she finally opened the door, she proved that she was a lousy actress. She stuttered worse than Joe and flitted about the room like the proverbial cat on a hot tin roof.

"What's wrong with you, b-b-baby?" asked Joe.

"Oh, I guess I've had too much sherry. I've been lonesome, honey, so I've been sitting by my little self and drinking."

Joe saw the bottle of sherry on the desk and then glanced past the bottle. "Drinking by yourself out of t-t-two glasses at the same time?"

"Oh gosh," she giggled nervously, "I must be going nuts."

"Why did you change your room, Loretta?"

"Some kind of phobia, I guess. I wanted to be closer to the street floor. You do screwball things when you're alone."

Joe picked a pipe up off the dresser and said, "You mean like smoking this?"

"Oh, that," she came back quickly. "That belongs to Hank Edwards. Hank left it in the lobby over a week ago, and the clerk asked me would I return it to him when I see him."

"It's a f-f-fine pipe," commented Joe. "It stayed s-s-smoking hot for over a week."

"Oh, come now, Joe," she coaxingly said. "Don't be jealous of Mr. Edwards; he's married."

"Right now I wish we were m-m-married so I could have the pleasure of suing you for divorce."

"Joe, you're acting like a real meanie. Whatcha got in that cute package, a present for me?"

"Yeah, but ya ain't gonna get it. All you're gonna get from me is a big fat goodbye."

Ignoring the burn Joe was doing, she asked coyly, "What's in the package, Joe?"

"Toilet water," he replied venomously, "and that's where it's going. Right down the toilet."

"I don't like you anymore, Joe Frisco; you're nasty."

At that moment, for the first time, Joe noticed a door that led to an adjoining room. He turned to Loretta and said dramatically, "Goodbye, Miss t-t-two-timer." There was no reply. He repeated, "Goodbye, Loretta." He then walked across the room to the adjoining door, knocked loudly, then shouted:

"GOODBYE, HANK!"

That was the end of Joe Frisco and the Dixieland Five, assisted by Loretta McDermott and Hank Edwards. Without a moment's hesitation, he headed for the depot and hopped a train for New York. He didn't even bother saying goodbye to Mike Fritzel or Walter Meakin. Upon arrival in New York, he looked up agent Harry Fitzgerald. Harry had seen him at his best at Fritzel's and had expressed a desire to represent him. Within two weeks, Harry got him his big opportunity. Joe was billed as the famous jazz dance creator and booked to appear at Broadway's internationally popular Rector's. Here he made his debut, and here he laid a big egg. He expressed

"OH, LORETTA, HOW COULD YOU?"

it thus, "I was b-b-booked for four weeks but I lasted f-f-five minutes."

On his very first job without Loretta and the band, he drew eight violins and two long-haired cello players for jazz accompaniment. Even Fitzgerald agreed that the orchestral background sounded as if it belonged in a mortuary.

"You're right," said Joe. "They killed me on my introduction and buried me for a finish."

With Fitzgerald by his side, they headed for a bar. It was ten days before either of them emerged from the haze. During this week and a half, Joe relived a poem he occasionally used in his act: "When a guy's too drunk to think of his mother—there's no love better than one dead drunk for another."

There was a cabaret in Miami that had been having some success with a jazz band called the Louisiana Lo-Downs. In spite of the flop at Rector's, Harry Fitzgerald had seen Joe perform with the proper musical backing and was firmly convinced that he had a star on his hands. All this man needed was some good jazz music behind him. A long-distance call disclosed that the Rendezvous in Miami was run by two Chicagoans. One of the partners, Bill Rothstein, had seen Joe perform at Mike Fritzel's. He was not only interested but eager.

"You can buy him for a thousand dollars a week on a four-week deal," pressed Harry. "If you saw him in Chicago, you know you'll be buying a good attraction."

Mr. Rothstein now had his inning. "My partner just told me he saw Frisco at Rector's in New York and says he wouldn't give him a job as a busboy. My partner and I don't always agree. It so happens I'm a gambler, and I'm gonna lead with my chin. If your man wants four weeks down here at $750 a week, you got a deal."

Fitzie didn't try to deal. "I like your straight talk, Mr. Rothstein, and we accept your terms. Please send a wire of confirmation. And Mr. Rothstein, you wanna know something? Your partner will end up voluntarily giving Joe Frisco a bonus."

"Mr. Fitzgerald, do *you* wanna know something?" laughed Bill. "You're funnier than the guy you're booking."

Joe Frisco went to Miami for a four-week engagement and was such a big hit that he stayed four months. He spent his days at Hialeah Racetrack, but at night, when he wasn't performing, he brooded over Loretta. The torch was still burning.

Rothstein, a good showman, had a theory: "Never let the room get cold." In between shows, he always had some kind of entertainment going on. At this time, he had Sylvia Shore, a singer who played her own accompaniment on a little portable piano. She was a little on the plump side and obviously Jewish. Sylvia's type of singing was made to order for the Miami area. She had beautiful full tones and wailed a ballad with all the pathos of a cantor singing in a temple on the holy days.

Between shows each night Joe would disappear. He found his way to a corner on a little balcony from which the spotlights were worked. Here he would hide in the shadows while Sylvia sang "Are You Lonesome Tonight?" As she went on—"do you miss me tonight, are you sorry we drifted apart?"—Joe would listen intently, close his eyes, and load up with self-pity. When the song was over he would head right for the bar. The bartender was always ready for him with a double whiskey.

Rothstein observed Joe's behavior and worked out a plan. A Chinese prostitute was one of the Rendezvous's best patrons. She was young and attractive. Rothstein handed her a twenty-dollar bill and said, "I want you to take care of Mr. Frisco. Make him forget the broad that dumped him, understand? Do a good job, Kim, and you get another twenty. I know you're a real pro and I can depend on you. Now don't let me down."

Kim invited Joe to tea. He had a wonderful afternoon. Later, he explained to Bill, "I met her three sisters and her mother and they're all swell p-p-people. Only one thing I couldn't understand. They all called the m-m-mother Madam."

When Joe arrived back in New York, he had exactly eleven dollars. Fitzgerald was ready to throw the desk at him. He had not sent Harry one cent commission in the entire four months.

"What the hell kind of an ingrate are you?" yelled Harry. "You owe me twelve hundred dollars."

"Ain't I good for twelve hundred?" shot back Joe.

"You're good for nuthin'," his agent retorted. "Who took you for your bankroll, that bookmaker bum you palled with?"

"He's not a bum, Harry. He's sending his two children through c-c-college."

"You mean you're sending his two children through college. Sucker! I bet you didn't send your mother ten cents."

Joe's eyes filled, then he stammered shamefully, "I'm n-n-no goddamn g-g-good."

Harry, who was just as soft as Joe, shouted: "All right, knock off the sob stuff. Get some guts, buster, and listen carefully, because this is your last chance with me. I can book you for four weeks with Roy Mack in his new show at the Green Mill Gardens, in Chicago. After that—and only if you begin to act like a human being—I'm positive I will have a deal all locked up with Flo Ziegfeld. He's gonna do a new edition of the *Midnight Frolics* for the Roof Garden."

"Jesus, Harry, I'll make you proud of me, I swear. I been out of my mind for six months, b-b-but I got hold of myself now. When do I open in Chicago?"

"In three weeks," was Fitzie's reply, "and don't ask me what you're gonna do in the meantime because I figure it should take you at least three weeks to walk there. Also, don't ask me what you're gonna use for money, because you can rest assured you're not getting any from me."

Thanks to the Old Reliable, Grant Clarke, Joe missed no meals and reported to Roy Mack in plenty of time for his opening at the Green Mill Gardens.

Rasputin

The Green Mill Gardens was one of Chicago's most elaborate cabarets. The decor was luxurious, and generally the entertainment was of a quality that outclassed the other night spots in the area.

Roy Mack was the most experienced producer working out of Chicago. He had spent many years with Gus Edwards as actor and manager and later produced on his own. He knew not only his business but also his people and how to handle them. He was responsible for the rise of Joe E. Lewis at the Frolics, where he also produced the shows. Roy was fond of Frisco and familiar with his every idiosyncrasy.

With a huge assist from Rasputin, the opening night was a complete sellout. "Ras," a sort of public relations man without portfolio, knew every regular patron of the night spots. How he came to be called Rasputin was always a stumper. Russia's Rasputin was a holy man and a mystic. To the Russian czar and czarina and their subjects, he declared, "Only through me can ye hope to be saved." Many a nightclub operator was saved by Chicago's Rasputin. He admitted that the closest he ever got to Saint Petersburg was in Florida on his way to Sarasota. But like his counterpart, he had a certain power and could influence a lot of people.

On this night he did a fabulous job for the Green Mill Gardens. A sea of familiar faces was on hand to welcome Joe Frisco back to the Windy City. One face, however, was missing. When Joe acknowledged his ovation with teary eyes, the customers thought it was an emotional reaction to their enthusiasm. Rasputin knew better. He used to hang around with Frisco, and he knew Joe's every mood. He didn't claim to be a mystic, but intuitively he knew that time had not soothed Joe's hurt. So as a friend he labored tirelessly to find Loretta McDermott, but he couldn't find one single trace of her. She had evaporated.

It was a full-time job to keep Joe from having fits of depression. The audiences continued to be just as enthusiastic as they were on opening night, so at least while he was entertaining he had all his old-time zing. Backstage between shows, however, he was bored and he was boring. Something had happened to the dressing room comedian who used to keep the performers in stitches.

So dispirited was he that he wouldn't even take a gander at other pretty women. Producer Roy Mack always came up with the best-looking line of girls in Chicago. In this show he had sixteen gorgeous girls. He billed them as the "Sweet Sixteen Bathing Beauties." Joe showed no interest. He paid no more attention to these gals than he did to the BeeHee and Rubyatte troupe of tumbling Arabs. The captain of the sixteen cuties was quite a girl herself. She felt slighted by Joe's lack of interest. "What's the matter, Mr. Frisco?" she inquired. "Don't you like bathing beauties?"

"I dunno," replied Joe, "I never b-b-bathed any."

Roy Mack walked into the conversation just in time to enjoy the laugh. The girl wasn't amused. Turning to Roy, she said, "This character makes a profession of ignoring the opposite sex. His dressing room should be in an isolation ward."

"Honey," commented Mack, "the only females this guy bothers with are fillies and mares."

"Humph," she grunted as she walked away, "he must have some fine dates."

"Baby," responded Joe, "I can get in enough trouble in my own s-s-stable." He now turned to Mack. "Roy, ja b-b-bring me some moo?"

"Nope," was the curt reply. Being a compulsive horseplayer himself, Mack knew that if he advanced Joe any money, he'd head right for Arlington Park Racetrack. Joe was pouting, "You used to be my favorite, b-b-but you're just an also-ran now."

"I can't be your wet nurse, Joe. Get smart; tomorrow try mind betting. It's fun. Get a *Racing Form,* pick your horses, then make your bets mentally. You play the whole card just as if you were at the track, but instead of using money, you make the bets in your mind. Now you turn on the radio and listen to the race results. Try it tomorrow; it's a kick!"

The next afternoon Joe Frisco phoned Roy Mack. "I tried your betting system and did as you said: b-b-betting in my mind. The fourth race just finished and I'm b-b-broke—what do I do now?"

On the third week of the engagement, Joe was offered five hundred dollars to appear at a fifty-dollar-a-plate political fund-raising dinner. This appearance would constitute a breach of contract, but Roy Mack was willing to okay the engagement and even adjust his own time schedule under the following conditions: one hundred dollars would go to Joe's mother, a hundred to Grant Clarke, two hundred to Harry Fitzgerald, and the remaining one hundred dollars, Roy suggested, could be used by Joe to feed the horses. Joe agreed reluctantly.

Mack did a great service for Joe Frisco when he forwarded that two hundred dollars to Harry Fitzgerald. Harry had just about had it, as far as Joe Frisco was concerned. Now he got interested again and firmed the appointment for both of them to meet with Mr. Ziegfeld in the latter's office.

As a result of that meeting Joe Frisco became a star. On that opening night, Florenz Ziegfeld learned he had a success. I quote Al Jolson: "You ain't heard nuthin' yet."

Since the Ziegfeld *Midnight Frolic* on the New Amsterdam Roof was a late show, many of the working Broadway stars were able to get over in time to see Joe Frisco perform. A number of top name performers took the time to come backstage and visit with him in his dressing room. Fred Astaire, for one, was fascinated by Joe's dance style. After several visits, they kiddingly worked up a little routine in which they communicated through their feet. They danced out signals like two telegraph operators communicating in Morse code. Years later, Fred and Joe met in the Turf Club at Hollywood Park. Astaire's thoroughbred Triplicate was running that day. Joe hadn't seen Fred for twenty years, but at the racetrack Joe's greeting was always the same: "Who do you like in the b-b-big race?"

Gentle Fred Astaire was never one to press his opinion, especially at a racetrack. On this day, however, he said to Joe, "Listen," and he tapped out a rhythm on one foot. He then inquired of Joe, "Remember the code? Do you know what I spelled out?"

"T-T-Triplicate," replied Joe. "I saw him in his prep race. He should be p-p-pulling a plow."

Triplicate won and paid a big price. "What dya say now, Joe?" inquired Fred, jubilantly.

"I should be p-p-pulling a plow," was the sheepish reply.

Another of Joe's dressing room visitors was Jack Norworth, who wrote "Take Me Out to the Ball Game." Jack reciprocated by having Joe as his guest next day at Keith's Colonial Theatre. On the bill was Shelton Brooks. He, too, was a writer. Norworth observed that Frisco and Brooks were strangers. "You two have never met? Gawd, every night when you say your prayers, you should bless each other."

Frisco was befuddled; he didn't know this man had written "The Darktown Strutters' Ball." Brooks didn't know Frisco, but on this day his mind was far removed from "Strutters' Ball." He had just received a big juicy royalty check for his other hit song, "Some of These Days."

Covering his embarrassment, he said to Joe, humorously, "You wouldn't be Sophie Tucker, would you?"

"No," said Joe, "I just didn't wear my b-b-brassiere today."

Later, while Jack was in his dressing room changing back to street clothes, Joe stood in the wings and watched Smith and Dale in their hilarious comedy sketch, "Dr. Kronkhite."

Dale, the German doctor, was looking down Smith's throat. "Come now, say ah—ah—open, please—open wider, so—now again, say ah—ah—." Then again he looked into Smith's open mouth and exclaimed excitedly, "Ah ha, I knew it—knew it!"

"You knew vot?" pleaded Smith. "Vot iss it?"

"You need glasses," was the typical Dr. Kronkhite reply. Joe Frisco guffawed.

11

My Broadway

Every night during those first few weeks was like an opening night. In no time Joe knew everyone along the big street. He loved Broadway. He joined the Friars, an actor's club composed mostly of comedians. The types of comics were as varied as fingerprints. You might see Will Rogers or George Jessel, Ed Wynn or Milton Berle, or a baggy pants comic who would take a pratfall at a funeral just for a laugh.

The so-called Greek comedian "Parkyakarkus" described the Friars Club this way.

"The Friars is a difficult club to get into—you must either be a resident or a nonresident. You must be sponsored and vouched for by at least two men—who are listed in the phone book. These men investigate you, and sometimes these investigations drag on for—five or six minutes. If approved, the proposed member may then write a check and even then there is a wait—until the ink dries."

Joe Frisco never wrote a check. He always carried his inventory in his pocket. He paid cash.

Until now, Joe had enjoyed fame only as a hoofer. In no time at all after joining Ziegfeld's show, he became the comedian's funnyman. His wit was being repeated and was permeating Broadway. His first big laugh at the Friars Club came at the expense of suave Frank Fay, who was guest emceeing a show for the members. Joe's dance routine was a huge success. After Joe had taken several bows, Fay entered. The applause for Frisco continued unabated. Fay called Joe back. Again he bowed and then said, "Mr. Fay and g-g-gentlemen, I wanna say thanks for this warm welcome to the F-F-Friars."

Placing his hand on Joe's shoulder, Frank said, "Joe, as Broadway's adopted son, you're welcome to our family." The Friars applauded enthusiastically and Frank continued, "I don't find it difficult to embrace you, because you remind me of my uncle."

"You mean when I d-d-dance?" asked Frisco eagerly.

"No," said Fay, "when you talk."

Joe's juices started to ferment.

"No offense intended," said Fay, "but you do have a speech impediment, do you not?"

"Wr-wrong," said Joe, "I have no imp-p-pediment. I s-s-stutter."

The audience was amused, and Fay said, "Maybe it's a blessing—it helps you get laughs."

"Maybe you should s-s-stutter," snapped Joe.

The brother Friars laughed and then applauded. They sensed that Johnny Newcomer wasn't anybody's pushover. With this little encouragement Frisco became the aggressor. "You know, Mr. Fay, a man who s-s-stutters never speaks a hasty word."

"That's well put," agreed Fay and then said, patronizingly, "Lucky is the man who is pleased with himself."

"And who would know that b-b-better than you, Mr. Fay?"

Ignoring this crack, Frank continued the repartee. "Mr. Frisco, I know two famous physicians who run a clinic. A speech clinic. They're not only famous but reasonable, and they specialize in speech therapy."

Fearing he had been impolite, Joe asked, "What are their names?"

Gleefully Fay retorted, "Smith and Dale."

This unexpected double cross got a howl from the actor, so Fay added to it quickly, "When you go, ask for Dr. Kronkhite; they say he's good."

"He is," said Joe quickly. "He c-c-cured me!"

The audience howled, and Joe hung right there until the laughs started to wane. Then he walked toward the exit and said, "Mr. Fay, wipe the egg off your f-f-face!"

After having lived for years on coffee and doughnuts, Joe chose Billy LaHiff's Tavern on Forty-eighth Street for his hangout. One evening he was gorging himself with a porterhouse steak when the humorous Bugs Baer arrived.

"Hello, Joe," greeted Bugs; then looking around, he asked: "Where is everybody? The room is deserted."

"Yeah," replied Joe, "here I sit eating a s-s-six-dollar steak and there's n-n-nobody here to catch me."

A few minutes later, Damon Runyon joined Bugs and Joe. Runyon and

Bugs were always on the alert for a funny Frisco quote. It didn't take long for the occasion to present itself. Little Billy Rhodes arrived on the scene. The three-foot-tall midget sauntered over to the trio. Billy's chin just reached the tabletop. Frisco, who had been talking to Runyon, turned and seeing Little Billy's head on the table inquired casually, "Who sent for J-J-John the Baptist?"

Imitations of Joe became so common that B. F. Keith's Colonial Theatre had a Frisco dance contest. With "no smoking" signs all over the place, dozens of dancers were lighting matches and blowing sparks from cigars. Said Joe, "The fireman became the b-b-big attraction. He s-s-stopped the show."

With success, Joe crystallized a dream. A part of his weekly salary was assigned to a bank. This compulsory savings plan was to build a fund that would be used to build his mother a home in Dubuque. Knowing his inclination to procrastinate, he hoped that the plan would be irrevocable.

Ever popular with the guys at the club, he lived for laughs and stayed clear of any romantic involvements. Why he got half potted before he went to his hotel each night only Joe knew.

One day, a loved Friar died. While Lou Mosconi and Frisco were riding to the graveside at Cypress Hills Cemetery, they passed the Machpelah Cemetery. "Hey, look at that handsome mausoleum," said Lou. "See the name on it? Houdini! That's the famous escape artist, Harry Houdini. He was great."

"Yeah," agreed Joe, "but I'd like to see him escape from there."

After the funeral, the boys went back to the Friars. Joe forgot to eat but proceeded to drown his sorrow. When he tried to get down off the bar stool, his knees buckled. He looked like Rubber Legs Edwards. He grabbed hold of the bar for a moment and then gave a perfect imitation of Leon Errol. He listed like a sinking ship and looked as if he were walking on the side of a hill, but he made it to his hotel room.

He was sleeping soundly when at three A.M. the phone rang. He fumbled but finally found his ear. "Chicago calling, this is person-to-person, please. I want Joe Frisco."

Almost inaudibly, he repeated, "Chicago, whoziss?"

"Joe, it's Ras. Rasputin, Joe—Joe, I found her. Hello, Joe, do ya hear me?"

There was silence. Joe was trying hard to contain himself and shake out the cobwebs.

"Ras, w-w-where are ya? Er, I mean w-w-where is she? Oh, Ras, g-g-gimme twenty minutes. Call me back collect, Ras, will ya, p-p-please?" He hung up the phone, sat on the edge of the bed, and sobbed himself sober. Twenty minutes later the call came. Sixteen dollars later, Joe knew the whole story. Loretta was back in Chicago, broken in spirit and broke financially. She was sick and alone—and repentant. Oh, how she needed Joe.

Joe went as soft as a piece of butter exposed to the sun. He wired Rasputin three hundred dollars for fare and some new clothes. Now all that remained was to wait it out for two long weeks until Loretta McDermott arrived in New York. Joe went to meet her. When the two of them walked out of Grand Central Station, Loretta was snuggled against Joe, hanging onto his arm. All they needed to complete the tableau was the voice of Fannie Brice singing "My Man."

It was quite a contrast to the morning they pulled into Chicago's La Salle Street station at three A.M., exhausted, hungry, and discouraged. Now instead of each carrying a couple of suitcases, they hung on to each other while a redcap hung on to the luggage. When they reached the street, they didn't walk or take a street car or ride the el. A chauffeur was waiting with a big black limousine.

No doughnuts and coffee that night. It was lobster at the Astor. As they entered, the orchestra stopped the music and in recognition switched the tune to "The Darktown Strutters' Ball." The diners applauded, and Joe stood and took a polite bow. Loretta had learned of Joe's success, but what she saw on her first day in town eclipsed her wildest imagination.

"Joe, I'm thrilled for you; you know the gossip around Chicago is that you are making more money than President Harding."

"Why shouldn't I?" was the rejoinder. "He hasn't made good yet."

That night when Loretta sat out front and watched Joe perform, she decided that whatever Ziegfeld was paying him, it wasn't enough.

The first week back together was a real Cinderella story. It's hard to picture Joe Frisco as a Prince Charming; but Loretta was a very believable Cinderella. The glass slipper fit her perfectly. It came in the form of a ring with a diamond that Joe described as being as big as a grape. At any rate, it appeared that big to Loretta.

One Monday afternoon Loretta and Joe went to see an opening show at the Palace. Joe had never played the Palace, and Loretta had never seen it. To him, the Palace was the top of the mountain. An opening day there was as exciting as the Kentucky Derby. The audience was generally studded with stars, critics, agents, and layoffs. If you clicked at the Palace, never again did you have to scrounge around for the last half of a split week. On this particular week, the headline attraction was Eddie Foy and the Seven Little Foys. Joe Frisco was probably the only person Eddie Foy ever made cry. While the audience was enjoying the act, Joe was reliving the time he saw the name Foy on the marquee of the Dubuque Opera House. He remembered dancing in the streets for the crowds who stood in line, waiting to see the great comic in his hit show, *Over the River.*

Now, as the audience reacted hilariously to the Foy family, Joe was seeing in flashback his own youthful performance. Giant tears were rolling down his cheeks. He could see the faces of the folks in the crowd . . . he could hear the jingle of the coins as they hit the pavement . . . he could see the beautiful dancing shoes he had bought for those coins—and smell them burning in the potbellied stove. He shuddered when he thought of his dad's cruelty but felt ashamed of his own temper. He regretted not only that he had hit his father but also that he had run out on his mother without even a farewell embrace.

Thunderlike applause for the Foy family shook Joe back to reality. The act was finished. The seven kids were lined up on the stage taking a bow, and Joe, too, howled when the dad said, "It took me a long time to put this act together."

On that same show Pat Rooney and Marion Bent, a mixed team, had a peculiar effect on Loretta. Whether it was jealousy or envy, she lost no time in letting Joe know that just vicariously sharing his success was not enough.

"Joe," she pleaded, "aren't we ever gonna dance together again? Can't I even get to work with you when you play a benefit?"

Joe, ever kindhearted, rented a rehearsal room at the Lyric Theatre on Forty-second Street. For several hours each day, he and Loretta worked on double dance routines. Joe was getting just as big a bang out of it as he did when they put their first act together. She finally got back in the act at a police show benefit in Mount Vernon, New York. Joe boasted they were such a hit that "Loretta put back all the b-b-bows she had stolen in our early days."

On the way home from Mount Vernon they were stopped for speeding. Joe informed the motorcycle cop that they were just returning from a police benefit. He then showed the officer the gold engraved police whistle with which he had been presented. The officer forthwith told Joe just what he could do with the whistle.

"Well," reflected Joe, "it's g-g-good it wasn't a sheriff's benefit. They always give the actors a b-b-badge shaped like a s-s-star."

Before long, Joe, not surprisingly, felt underpaid. Against the wishes of Fitzgerald, Joe found his way to Ziegfeld's office. "Mr. Ziegfeld will see you now," announced the secretary. "Please make it brief, sir; my boss's schedule is very tight."

"So is your b-b-boss," flipped Joe.

Ziegfeld made it known quickly that he had some very definite rules. "Number one, I bought you as a single act, Mr. Frisco. You have been a success and I never tamper with success. You are under contract until May fifteenth and until that date you will continue as a single, sir. That is definite. Number two, I do not engage sweethearts or man-and-wife teams. They're double trouble."

In a futile attempt to be funny, Joe said, "Mr. Ziegfeld, on May sixteenth I'll still love you but I won't be with you!"

"Joe," said Ziggy, "you're a good entertainer, but apparently success is too difficult for you to handle."

The big producer then stood up. Even Joe knew that when an executive stands up behind his desk, the interview is over. Joe started for the door, but Ziegfeld had more to say.

"Someday you will appreciate that the season spent under the banner of Ziegfeld was a big feather in your cap."

Always reaching for laughs, Joe couldn't resist, "I'll p-p-put that feather where I sit, Mr. Ziegfeld, and I'll f-f-fly home. Thanks for the t-t-transportation."

The Winchell word that Ziegfeld and Frisco had "pfft" got around more quickly than scuttlebutt in an army camp.

Harry Fitzgerald washed his hands of Joe Frisco. He would have no more to do with him. He knew he had made a costly decision, but he argued, "Some things are more important than money. I can't tolerate irresponsibility."

Agent Jack Curtis was delighted to fill Fitzgerald's shoes, and Eddie Darling, chief booker for the Palace, was even more eager to buy an attraction that could flaunt the Ziegfeld badge of quality. Frisco was signed as soon as his name was offered. Darling had Curtis bring Joe to the office of vaudeville's kingpin, E. F. Albee, for some publicity photographs. The newspaper release showed Frisco being presented with a pen while sitting with Albee at the latter's desk. The caption was "Mr. Albee tells Joe Frisco to write his own ticket."

Joe confided later, "I may not know how to write, b-b-but I know how to count." In 1927, Joe's salary for the Palace was twenty-five hundred dollars a week. As Joe and Curtis walked out of the Palace Theatre building, they had to walk over some loose planks that covered an excavation.

"Wonder what the hell they're digging here?" asked Jack as he stumbled over the raised end of a board.

"Mr. Albee's grandchild lost his baseball," cracked Joe.

After shouting goodbye to Jack Curtis, Joe walked briskly to the Friars Club. Like any actor, he was anxious to tell someone, anyone, that he had just been booked for the Palace. He ran into Eddie Foy Sr., who wasn't even sure who Joe was and couldn't care less. Joe bent old man Foy's ear about his career and concluded by saying, "Before I open at the P-P-Palace, they want me to play a week in Newark. Do you think p-p-playing Newark will hurt me?"

"Naw," drolled the elder Foy. "It won't hurt you, but it might hurt Newark."

Foy then hastened out of the club so he wouldn't be late for his matinee—in Newark.

Joe added to the act—along with Loretta—Cliff Edwards, known later as Ukulele Ike, to augment the musical combo. Cliff played drums and was great on the uke. He also had an unusual voice. He took a very small salary from Frisco because he was intent on being seen at the Palace. His rise as an entertainer proved that his judgment was sound. Everybody soon knew Ukulele Ike, and later he won lasting fame as the off-screen voice for Walt Disney's Jiminy Cricket.

The act went beautifully at Newark, but the following Monday Joe got a slight attack of "Palacitis." This is an occupational disease that has never been listed in a medical publication. It manifests itself just before your first appearance at the Palace Theatre. The first symptoms are fluttering in your stomach and acute attacks of indigestion and heartburn, accompanied by shortness of breath. Palacitis can be cured only by making your first entrance onstage. Joe was so tense at breakfast that he couldn't even swallow a dunked doughnut. When they called, "Five minutes," his knees felt as though they were going to buckle. At last, his name flashed on the enunciator. Conductor Benny Roberts gave the downbeat for the musical introduction, and in a jiffy Joe Frisco was on stage. Almost instantly, the audience surrendered. Frisco was in and over.

Sime Silverman, editor of *Variety*, concluded a lengthy rave notice with "This man has arrived. He's a star."

Zit, the Broadway critic, reviewed a vaudeville show like a horse race. He used a chart like the *Racing Form*, showing post position and who ran first, second, and so on. Zit called Frisco an easy winner, a thoroughbred who completely outclassed the entire field.

The word of Joe's success at the Palace that week spread like a summer fire. The demand for his act was so great that he was wanted in a dozen places at the same time. He started what they used to call bicycling (playing two theatres during the same week), but Joe was unable to take too much of that. The booking office kept him around New York for many months.

When the time finally arrived for him to make a tour of the hinterlands, Joe was not happy. He loved Broadway.

"Boy," he complained, "as soon as you leave N-N-New York every town is B-B-Bridgeport."

Indianapolis annoyed him. "That audience," he commented, "sounded like they were applauding with their knees. I don't think they ever took off their g-g-gloves."

At the Davis Theatre in Pittsburgh, he found a receptive audience, but after every show Mr. Connelly, the manager, would warn him to "keep it clean."

Said Joe, "He keeps asking me to k-k-keep it clean and outside the stage door the snow is black from c-c-coal dust, the white curtains in the hotel are gray, the d-d-drinking water is tan. And the m-m-manager says to k-k-keep it clean!"

The road tour was a bore until Philadelphia. Joe loved the City of Brotherly Love because every night he commuted to New York. The following week at Atlantic City was also a good week. He was on the bill with Eddie Foy and the Seven Little Foys. Here Charlie Foy and Joe struck up a friendship that endured for the rest of their lives.

After a return to the Palace Theatre and return dates at all the New York two-a-day theatres, Joe undertook a tour of the Orpheum Circuit. This gave him a chance to visit his mother and family for one day. When the prodigal son arrived back in Dubuque, there was no fanfare or pageantry. He showered his mother with gifts, but the general picture was dismal. Again he pledged that he was going to build her the finest home in Dubuque.

The Orpheum Circuit was more like a sightseeing tour, and Joe was not what we used to call a scenery snatcher. He was pure unadulterated ham and was unhappy until he hit San Francisco, always a great show town. The audiences at the San Francisco Orpheum were reminiscent of the Palace. Next stop was the Orpheum in Los Angeles. Here the auditorium was full of silent movie stars. They were a tremendously demonstrative audience. It was a kick for him to look out front and see Douglas Fairbanks, Dolores Del Rio, Francis X. Bushman, Harold Lloyd, and Polly Moran, to name just a few.

Visiting the movie sets, Joe watched Rudolph Valentino break the heart of Natasha Rambova while three tired musicians created the mood by playing "Hearts and Flowers." He met Mary Pickford, Fatty Arbuckle, and Charlie and Syd Chaplin, but he was delighted when the train headed back toward New York.

Contracts had been signed for Joe to appear in Earl Carroll's *Vanities* (1928). Alongside Joe as he walked into the Carroll Theatre for the first time was Dave Chasen, in those days a stooge in the act of Broadway star Joe Cook. Overhead, in fancy print, was the line that helped make Carroll famous. Dave, the now highly regarded Hollywood restaurateur, read it aloud.

"Through these portals walk the most beautiful girls in the world."

"Gee," kidded Joe, "I m-m-must be coming in the wrong entrance. Are these the gals that b-b-bathe in champagne?"

"That was a publicity stunt," said Dave, pointing to a life-size image of W. C. Fields, "but they say that guy bathes in whiskey and soda."

In several weeks, the *Vanities* played Atlantic City before opening in New York. W. C. Fields and Joe appeared together in several scenes. After each scene, Fields would complain about Joe's stuttering. "It's a put-on," Bill would wail, "a cheap low-down trick to try to steal my thunder."

Their friendship soured, and they stopped talking to one another. On opening night in New York they shared a dressing room. They sat side by side, each staring into the same huge makeup mirror. Both had opening night jitters; each ignored the other. Just before the opening overture, Joe received a telegram. He eagerly ripped it open. The message embarrassed him. It read: "Good luck on your opening tonight!" It was signed: W. C. Fields.

Joe looked into the big mirror and said, "Tell Bill I w-w-wish him luck, too, and I hope he'll be as b-b-big a hit as, er, I am."

"Listen, my boy," snarled Fields, "I've juggled Indian clubs for a living, I've imitated Teddy Roosevelt, and I've played street fakers and pitch men. I thought I knew all the tricks; but you're a bigger faker in life than the characters I've played."

After the show, Fields stepped into a drugstore and there sat Joe using the phone. Bill eavesdropped, and when Joe hung up, W. C. fairly bellowed, "I knew it, you phony. I heard every word you said and you didn't stutter once."

Joe puffed his cigar, then flicked the ashes, looked up into Bill's kisser, and said, "I was t-t-talking long distance."

These two needled one another for a full season. When the show closed, Joe had the urge to return to vaudeville. This time, Joe added, besides Loretta, Eddie Cox to the act. Cox was a fine song-and-dance man. He and Joe did a soft-shoe dance together that was a sure clincher. At the Palace the act again got fine notices, except from one critic, Walter Winchell, the last guy Joe dreamed would throw scallions in his direction. Winchell said of Loretta, "This gal belongs in a Chicago honky-tonk."

That same night Joe was scheduled to sit on the dais at a testimonial dinner at the Friars Club honoring Winchell. Frisco phoned Winchell and informed him that Loretta had joined the army of violent Winchell haters. "Walter," he stated flatly, "I won't b-b-be at your dinner tonight. If I show up for you, I lose her."

Winchell wouldn't believe it: "You gotta be kidding, Joe."

"I'm not," was the reply. "She's prettier, and I like her better."

"Do you mean you would let down all your friends because as an honest critic I expressed my opinion of Loretta?"

"It took her ten years to become a dancer," philosophized Joe. "It takes only ten minutes to become a critic."

"You just loused up a good quote. Now please don't louse up my dinner tonight. I need you there, Joe."

"Where will I tell Loretta I'm going?" he asked, softening.

"Oh, tell her you're going to Polly Adler's house."

"Good idea," replied Joe, enthusiastically.

"Joe," said Walter in a kinder tone, "that's a whorehouse."

"I know," grinned Joe. "If I would ditch Winchell for P-P-Polly, Loretta would be so p-p-pleased, she'd open a ch-ch-charge account for me there." Joe attended the dinner.

As the week at the Palace wore on, Joe's momma complex overtook him again. He demanded a week's vacation to go to Dubuque. Curtis convinced the booking office to cooperate. After the Palace, he would play two more weeks in New York, then have a one-week layoff, followed by a week at the Majestic Theatre in Chicago.

Fenn Generaux, a well-known New York architect, was very fond of Joe. He volunteered to accompany him to Dubuque and help formulate all of Joe's plans. As he expressed it, "My fee will be the enjoyment of your company." Generaux had a Cadillac and a chauffeur and suggested that it might be fun to drive west. After driving for two days, they arrived in Chicago at two A.M. As they entered the Sherman House, the charwomen were cleaning the lobby. Against the wall stood a life-size photo of bandleader Abe Lyman. Stacked up in front of Abe's picture were at least a dozen large, highly polished brass cuspidors. Frisco took one look and declared, "Gee, Abe has a swell b-b-band but what did he do to get all these loving cups?"

Next day in Dubuque, Fenn helped purchase a lot and started to make a reality of Joe's plan for building his mother's dream house. A local contractor was hired, and the project got started immediately. The work proceeded in complete secrecy.

Joe's reunion with his mother, however, was disappointing. Mother Joseph was timid and absent-minded. On several occasions she called Joe "Charles," and the shock was demoralizing. Joe had reserved a suite at the Palmer House. He wanted more than anything to have his mom see him in action at the Majestic Theatre. But the very mention of spending a week in Chicago frightened her. She clung to Joe and melted with affection, but he couldn't get her to go for even a ride in the car. She was content to just sit with him on the couch and run her fingers through his hair. His sister, Mae, tried to convince her that a change would do her good, but the answer was no, and she remained adamant.

When Joe arrived back in Chicago, he was sad and dejected. He found Loretta and then called Eddie Cox, and over a bottle of bourbon, they discussed the act before retiring. The response at the Majestic was terrific. Joe, however, was feeling down in the dumps. He was ham enough to enjoy being a hit but equally depressed over being denied the joy of having his mother share the glory. At the stage door Joe was mobbed by old friends. Old reliable Rasputin was on hand, and before he could even shake his head no, he and the others were whisked to the Frolics Cafe, where they watched Joe E. Lewis do his show. At the conclusion, Joe E. lifted a glass from a ringside table. "A toast," he said. "First, always, to the red wine and brew; then, Joe Frisco, I drink to you."

The audience applauded until Joe Frisco took a bow. Joe E. then held up his hand for quiet. "Ladies and gentlemen, Joe's contract at the theatre prohibits any outside appearances. I'm sorry."

"Thanks, Joe," shouted Frisco, "and thanks for the toast, but next time make it steak."

Joe and Loretta danced till the wee hours, and Rasputin hung right on to them. He drove them back to the hotel, and after Loretta retired to her room, he and Frisco gabbed like two old maids. Ras finally fell asleep on the couch in Joe's suite. Next morning the hotel manager phoned to say that there would be an extra charge for the guest who shared the room. "That's okay," consented Joe, "but now send up an extra Gideons B-b-bible."

The dwindling days of the Roaring Twenties had arrived, and the roar certainly echoed through show business. Vaudeville was fading rapidly. When Joe reached Los Angeles on this tour, he found that half of the Friars Club had moved to Hollywood. Charlie Foy's elder brother Bryan, who produced *Lights of New York,* the first all-talking movie, was a highly regarded man on the Warner Brothers staff. He hosted Joe the entire week. Together they visited the various studios, saying hello. Joe's humor convulsed the actors working on the sets, and Foy was delighted over Joe's welcome because he too was having a swell time. Joe called Bryan's brother Charlie in New York. "Brynie is really taking care of me, day in and n-n-night out."

Six weeks later, in Kansas City, Joe got word that the house that was being built for his mother was progressing nicely. Immediately, he started buying things and shipping them to the Dubuque Van and Storage Company.

In Saint Louis an art dealer got Joe all excited over a painting of the Last Supper. The asking price was $250. "T-t-too high," was the complaint. They haggled, and when the dealer dropped the price clear down to $150, Joe complained again. "A hundred and fifty dollars for 'The Last Supper'? No dice! T-t-tell you what: I'll give ya t-t-ten dollars a plate."

The dealer laughed hysterically, and Joe got the painting for his price. After playing a week in Pittsburgh, the act was booked for another week in Pennsylvania, but it was a split week—the first half at Easton, and Thursday, Friday, and Saturday in Bethlehem. It took only two days in Easton to make Joe miserable. On Wednesday morning he called his agent in New York. "I'm not going to play Bethlehem," he shouted through the phone. "G-g-get another act, because I'm w-w-walking."

"You better not walk," was the first retort. The agent then chewed Joe's ear off, concluding with, "If you know what's good for you, you'll fulfill your contract."

"D-d-damn it," shouted Joe, "Christ walked out of B-B-Bethlehem—why can't I?"

On Saturday night, Joe informed Loretta and Eddie that he was going to hop into New York for Sunday. "I'll see you at the theatre Monday morning in Phillie." Joe's visit to New York was marred by heavy rain. He caught a cold and had a bad case of sniffles. He spent most of the day in bed. It was now after seven o'clock and he had just sat down to have dinner at the Friars Club when in walked George Jessel.

"Hello, Joe," greeted George. "This is indeed a surprise—you're the last guy I expected to run into today. Haven't you read the morning paper?"

"No, d-d-did I miss something?"

"Hell, yes," said Jessel excitedly, "apparently you did." He reached for the "bulldog" edition of the morning paper, placed it on the table in front of Frisco, and said, "Get a load of this!"

Joe didn't have to read to see a large photo of Loretta and Eddie Cox. In bold type underneath it said: "Just Married."

Frisco couldn't believe his eyes. He went limp. He was unable to utter a sound or hold back a few uncontrollable tears—but just for a moment. He then reverted to character and started reaching for laughs.

"Georgie, if I had your talent I'd write a song, d-d-dedicate it to Eddie Cox, and entitle it, 'You P-p-put Me on My Feet When You T-t-took Her off My Hands.'"

Joe then took another look at the paper. He pondered over what he saw, shook his head, and tried again to be funny. "I leave 'em alone for one day and what happens? He gets a wife and I get a c-c-cold."

"It only proves one thing," said Jessel, philosophically. "Ya never can tell about a woman."

"And even if you can—you shouldn't," added Mr. Funnyman.

Jessel laughed but then insisted on being serious. "Joe, most people will congratulate the bride and groom, but I wanna congratulate you. You've got intestinal fortitude, guy. I know you love Loretta and I know how big a shock this is to you, so I must compliment you. I am proud of the way you control your wrath."

"Well," Joe reflected, and now he too got serious, "once, when I was a kid, I got hurt and lost my temper. I g-g-got violent and behaved like a g-g-goat and I've regretted it all my life. Now, again," he meditated, shook his head, and pointed to the photograph in the paper, "I am hurt—but doubly this time. I lose my girl and a guy I thought was my best friend."

"The sad part," cut in Jessel, "is that just as he doubled-crossed you, so eventually he will cross her."

"True," sighed Joe, "but m-m-maybe she's got it coming to her. Tomorrow morning in Philadelphia, when I meet Eddie, I would like to extend my congratulations by g-g-giving him a good stiff kick—you know where—but I feel he is more to be p-p-pitied than ruptured."

"And just what are you going to tell the fair damsel?" asked Jessel.

"Well, she likes to sleep late. Every morning I used to go in the coffee shop and pick up coffee and doughnuts to take to her room. Tomorrow, I'll knock on her door, show her this newspaper clipping and say, 'Just for this, you get no coffee and doughnuts.'"

"Stop clowning, Joe. Everyone has some romanticism in him."

"George, you got me mixed up with that lover with the big nose."

"You mean Cyrano de Bergerac," suggested Jessel, proudly.

"Well, I didn't mean Durante. But George, if you wanna know for real, I'm gonna s-s-skip the sentimental stuff. I wish her luck; after all, we s-s-started together. But she's got to know that now I laugh when I think I cried over her."

Incidentally, Joe Frisco claimed that George Jessel remembered that line and later used it as a title and theme for his hit song, "Oh How I Laugh When I Think How I Cried over You."

The reunion of the trio at Keith's Chestnut Street Theatre in Philadelphia was less than cordial.

"Sorry, Joe, you weren't here for our wedding," said Cox. "We would like to have had you as our best man."

"If I was the b-b-best man, Loretta wouldn't have m-m-married you." From then on, Joe would have no part of Mr. and Mrs. Eddie Cox, even though they continued to work for him in his act.

12

This Gorilla Was a Killer

Alone now and with much time on his hands, Joe became a pretty good nipper. A *Racing Form* and a bottle were his pacifiers. If he couldn't find a local bookmaker to get a bet down, he'd phone a bet in long-distance. Because of his betting, he succeeded in consistently losing his earnings and became delinquent in meeting the payments for his mother's house.

At this time, a most fortunate wire came from Hollywood. The Warner studio was casting a picture called *The Gorilla.* Bryan Foy, having sold Warner on Joe, wired Frisco an offer. Joe shot back a wire asking assurance that he would be the principal character.

For once Joe Frisco was topped. Brynie wired, "The principal character will be played by a real gorilla."

Loretta and Eddie Cox were given six weeks' notice that the act would dissolve. The seventh week, Joe Frisco arrived in the cinema capital. He was met by Brynie, two photographers, and a publicity man.

Joe had a reservation at the Plaza Hotel on Vine Street, but Foy nixed this quickly. "I've rented a home for you on North Foothill Road in Beverly Hills. Jimmie Starr has told the whole world in his column that you're getting forty gees for four weeks' work. Ya gotta go first cabin, Joe."

"What'll I d-d-do with a big house—and if I live in Beverly Hills, where will I find a b-b-bookmaker?" asked Joe.

"On your doorstep," replied Foy.

On the way to Beverly Hills, Brynie told Joe that he had advertised for a cook for him and that the studio would supply a car and a chauffeur for the first week.

Later, while Joe was luxuriating in a big overstuffed chair, the door chimes rang. "Sounds like Saint Patrick's Cathedral," commented Joe, as he went to open the door. There stood a beautiful girl in a silk, slinky maid's uniform. She was so pretty, she looked like Billie Dove with a suntan.

"I came for an interview with Mr. Frisco. I am a cook, and I am applying for the job of cooking for him."

Joe took another look and said, "I'm Mr. Frisco. You don't need to cook for me, honey. Come in—I'll c-c-cook for you!"

Joe had three days in which to learn his script, and since Foy was the director as well as Joe's benefactor, he journeyed out to visit with Joe that first night.

"Tell me," asked Frisco, "have I got a good fat part?"

Foy turned four or five pages and as he handed over the open script, he pointed and said, "There it is!"

Joe, who still couldn't read, looked at the open page and said, "Damn if it ain't."

Next morning bright and early, Foy had a dialogue director out at the house breathing down Frisco's neck. While he was trying to make Joe memorize lines, the radio was blasting the race results from Eastern tracks. By two o'clock, instead of the director teaching Joe to read the script, Joe had taught the director how to read a *Racing Form*.

If Joe had been as big a hit with the audience as he was with the people on the set, *The Gorilla* would have outgrossed *Gone with the Wind*. But the people on the set were laughing for the wrong reason. He missed every cue, fluffed every line, and was late for every entrance. Foy tried using cue cards, but not until the boy held the card upside down did he realize that Joe couldn't read. In one scene Joe was supposed to come up from the basement and push open a door, but he never arrived. Brynie shouted, "Cut—where the hell is Frisco?" Then, opening the door himself, he found Frisco sitting on the steps reading a scratch sheet.

"Sorry," apologized Joe, "I n-n-never heard the cue."

"You mean you didn't hear the gun go off?" asked a skeptical Foy. "What do you want me to do, use a cannon? Look, if you can't hear well, here's what we'll do. After you hear the gunshot—and you'll hear it this time—count to four. Ya got me? Four—then walk up the two steps and briskly push open the door." Again Director Foy shouted "Roll 'em." The boy stepped in with the clapboard. Foy shouted, "Take!" The scene started;

then with a terrific bang came the gunshot. They waited; again no Frisco.

"Where the hell are you now?" yelled Foy. "I asked you to count to FOUR—not FORTY!"

Now Joe was exasperated. "Damn it," he shouted, "I couldn't c-c-count any f-f-faster. You know I s-s-stutter."

They did these scenes so many times that when the number of takes was recorded, it was more like a tote board at the racetrack. The misadventures continued, and after the scheduled four weeks, it was necessary to add two more. Joe simply couldn't adjust. After being such a success as an entertainer, owing to his own creative sense, he found it difficult to take direction.

Bert Hanlon, a fine entertainer, humorist, and songwriter, visited the set. He had much in common with Joe. Though Bert was an extremely brilliant and well-read man, he would have gotten much more satisfaction out of sweeping the card at Santa Anita than having been given Jolson's part in *The Jazz Singer*.

"Ya know, Bert," Joe confided after blowing his lines for the fourth time, "the m-m-money out here is g-g-great, but I don't think I could take Hollywood for a s-s-steady diet."

"Joe," replied Bert, "my advice to you is don't buy anything out here that you can't pack in the back of your car."

"Are you telling me I haven't g-g-got a chance of m-m-making it in this p-p-picture business?"

"I didn't say that," cracked Bert, "but if I were you, I wouldn't be so careless about throwing away those half-smoked cigar butts."

Bert's remarks got Joe to thinking. The next day he sent a full week's salary to his brother-in-law in Dubuque. This was to take care of back payments, fines, liens, and other attachments in connection with the completion of his mother's home. With his conscience clear again, Joe got right back in the groove. He started betting on horses at every track in the country. One morning a strange bookmaker came to the door.

"Good morning, Mr. Frisco, my name is Leo. Here is today's scratch sheet. Please note the new phone numbers, because I'll be taking your bets starting today."

"What happened to my regular bookie?" inquired Joe.

"Oh, we started gambling with each other last night. He beat the socks off me playing gin rummy, and I quit. Then Connie flashed a pair of dice. That was his mistake. I won you in the crap game."

When the shooting of *The Gorilla* was over, Frisco should have changed his post office address. He lived at Del Mar Racetrack. There he hibernated until the morning Bryan Foy invited him to Santa Barbara to see a sneak preview of *The Gorilla.* Joe had no alternative but to acquiesce, though he felt like he was going to his own execution. Upon arrival at the theatre in Santa Barbara, Brynie and Joe chose two seats in the last row. After careful observation, Joe got the impression that Brynie was not looking forward to this preview with any more enthusiasm than he was.

"Would you like me to get you a C-C-Coke?" asked Joe.

"No thanks. If you wanna know the truth, right now I think I'd rather have a Mickey Finn," said Foy.

Eventually, after what seemed like an eternity, the curtains parted and on the screen flashed, "Warner Brothers Pictures presents—*The Gorilla*—starring Joe Frisco." It kicked off like a nightmare, dreamed up out of a book of horrors. As the epic went on, Joe slid down in his seat, lower and lower, until he was practically sitting on his collarbone. As he slipped lower and lower, his temperature rose higher and higher. During the entire running of the film Joe made only one remark, "Phew, it's hard to t-t-tell me from the gorilla." At last came the finish and, with twitchy fingers, Joe popped a phenobarbital into his mouth to deaden his jumpy nerves. When they reached the sidewalk, Joe turned to Brynie and said, "Well, Mr. Foy, I just m-m-made two pictures at once. My f-f-first and l-l-last."

The Gorilla is still in a can on a shelf. Probably the Society for the Prevention of Cruelty to Animals wouldn't let the proud possessors release it. Joe made one last visit to Del Mar to say goodbye to his money. He bid a fond adieu to many friends, including several trainers and jockeys. Little Nickie Wall, pointing to the beautiful view surrounding the racetrack, said, "You mean you're going back to rain and wind and sleet and leaving all this behind? This mild climate and exquisite scenery? I'm not working for the Chamber of Commerce, Joe, but look at how beautiful the hills are in the background."

"Yeah," retorted Joe, "but you can't put k-k-ketchup on them."

Chicago again greeted Joe with open arms. Rasputin was on hand, as usual, to see that Joe had a big opening. True, the weather was cold, but the welcome for Joe in the Windy City was always warm. His stories kidding himself about his short career as a movie star gave him a whole new approach. Joe concluded a long-run engagement the week before Christmas. The timing was perfect. He could now spend Christmas in Dubuque with his mother. This would be the first Christmas with Mom since he was a child. He spent days shopping in his feverish desire to play Santa Claus.

When he got off the train in Dubuque, he was laden down with Christmas-wrapped packages. The cab driver helped him up the snow-covered path with his bundles, then set the luggage on the steps and left. Holding all the bundles in his arms, Joe pressed the doorbell with his elbow. There was no response. He tried again. When there was no reply the third time, Joe set down the bundles and tried the knob. The door opened.

"Hello," he shouted, "hello, Mom?" Not a sound. Frantically, he rushed through the hall into the house, and there, sitting in a comfortable-looking overstuffed chair, in a warm cozy room, was his mother.

"Momma, Momma," he shouted repeatedly. "Momma, it's me, Momma." He sat on the arm of the chair and embraced and kissed her, but there was no response. At first he thought she was dead; then he realized that her face and body were warm. She moved her hands and her head, and he came to the realization that something was tragically wrong.

He kissed her hand and sobbed violently, but his mother was completely oblivious to his presence. Again he ran through the house. "Hello," he kept shouting, "where is everybody?" He could tell the house was being lived in, but no one, quite obviously, was looking after his mother. He waited, it seemed, an eternity. At long last, the front door opened and Joe's sister, Mae, entered carrying bags full of groceries. Joe soon learned the whole story. The poor guy didn't even know what the word *senile* meant. When he heard that his mother had suffered two strokes, he started asking questions. He was dismayed that she never even knew she had moved into a new house.

Mae assured him that mother was no longer conscious of any pain or suffering. "Joe," she pleaded affectionately, "don't be offended that we spared you from sharing the misery; there was nothing that could be done for Mom."

Joe's reaction was typical of his behavior when in trouble. He could never endure suffering, and as soon as possible he would again run away.

His sister sensed his helplessness and decided to ease his embarrassment. She assured him he could be of no help in the Joseph household. He quickly apologized for not having time to stay longer. Truth is, not until he reached the depot did he start to think over where he would go.

He headed for the Sherman House in Chicago, where he holed up for several days trying to get consolation out of a bottle. Whether Hialeah Park drew him, or the cold wind blew him, Miami was the next stop. Joe Frisco could book more engagements at a racetrack than most entertainers could in an agent's office. In no time, Joe was working and back in the old routine: the racetrack during the day and the club at night. He had become a master at table-hopping and elbow bending.

At the close of the season in Florida, he moved on to New York. There was always a spot for him at Club 18. It was fun working with Jack White, Pat Harrington, Frankie Hyers, Jackie Gleason, and Roy Sedley.

One day his friend Jack Pepper sold him on returning to California. Jack was booked for the Chi-Chi Club in Palm Springs. The owner had mentioned long-distance that he wished he could get Joe Frisco. Pepper, a pretty good horseplayer in his own right, said, "It's a wonderful life there, Joe. In the morning, while you're lolling around the swimming pool, a bookmaker comes with the *Racing Form* and takes your bets. You can bet on any racecourse in the country and get track odds. We'll stay at Bert Wheeler's joint, the Lone Palm. Everybody you meet there is from show business. You can bask in the sun and have a wonderful vacation—and all the time you're getting paid for it."

When they pulled into the driveway of the Lone Palm, six or seven men were being entertained by a dog that had unearthed what looked like a bone. Growling and tossing it up in the air, playfully holding it between its paws and chewing on it, the dog finally attempted to bury it again.

Frisco and Pepper walked toward the scene, amazed. "What's playing here?" asked Jack.

"Oh God," Lou Costello hilariously groaned, "poor Bob Woolsey. His lower denture disappeared over three weeks ago, and all the time this little mongrel had it buried."

"One thing is positive," said Joe, "the d-d-dog is enjoying Woolsey's lower m-m-more than I do mine."

"Another thing is positive," said Lou Costello, as he extended a welcome hand; "Joe Frisco always has a funny line when he makes his entrance. It's good to see you both. Do you guys know King Charney?"

Charney, a handsome, well-dressed man, extended his hand and said, "Welcome, gentlemen, I'm the new proprietor of the Lone Palm. Your accommodations are ready, and I'll be pleased to show you your rooms."

As they followed Charney, they had to walk past the pool. Joe was beside himself with joy. The first guys he saw reclining poolside were practically all horseplayers.

"Is this sumpin'?" nudged Pepper. "Take a gander; there's Durante, Jolson, Harry Akst, and hey, there's Leo Fitzgerald. Did you know he's the one and only agent Bert Wheeler ever had?"

"Maybe that's why Bert had to sell this joint," commented Frisco. "There's B-B-Bill Smith with Harry Ritz."

"Who's Bill Smith? "inquired Jack.

"Don't you know Bill? He was m-m-married to Ethel Merman for about f-f-five minutes. He took along a *Racing Form* on his honeymoon. She was looking for love, and he was looking for winners. Ya gotta meet him; he's a nice guy."

"Here you are, fellers," said Charney. "Rooms 117 and 118. I purposely put you on the back side of the house because I know you'll be working late and you'll want to sleep in the morning. Back here you're away from Jolson."

"You mean Jolson is noisy?" asked Pepper.

"Well," King explained, "Al wakes up early every morning, can't sleep, and has a bad habit of walking out to the pool and vocalizing. Do you like Al's singing?"

"Not at s-s-seven o'clock in the morning," was the hurried response.

"The Ritz Brothers are trying to cure him. Soon as he sings, they open their doors and shout, "EVERYBODY UP—JOLSON'S UP!"

"That wouldn't discourage Jolson," said Jack.

"Not Al," added Joe. "Instead of t-t-taking offense, he p-p-probably takes bows."

Opening night at the Chi-Chi Club was like old home week. There were so many famous names in the celebrity-packed room that at the finish Joe said, "With my s-s-stuttering, if I introduce all the stars that are here tonight, it will take me until Tuesday and I don't want to miss Lum and Abner, so g-g-good night."

The next day while others were having lunch, Jack and Joe had breakfast poolside. They couldn't believe their eyes. There were enough comics sitting around the pool to call a meeting of the Hollywood Comedy Club. Harry Ritz was taking pratfalls off the springboard, and some old guy kept goosing a waitress with his cane. At first they thought it was Lou Holtz, but it turned out to be the father of the Ritz Brothers, a cute old guy and mischievous as hell. Lou Costello had just blitzed Durante in a gin game. Jimmy paid off and complained to Frisco, "He beats me—and then this Charney guy takes it away from him." At that moment, Charney came along and added, "And then Jake here takes it away from all of us." Jake was Jake Katleman, the top banana in the gambling business in Palm Springs. He was a real swell guy who later took over the Rancho Vegas Hotel in Las Vegas. With him went Frank Portnoy and also Carl Choen, who later became casino manager of the Sands Hotel. They helped make Las Vegas America's playground.

Betting horses in Palm Springs was a strange experience for Joe. No jockeys around, no touts, no horse owners, and no trainers. All the poor guy had going for him was the *Racing Form*. Know what? He won over three hundred dollars the first week.

At the Chi-Chi Club he drew big, appreciative crowds. He knew most of the customers. The Springs at that time was Hollywood's most popular retreat. Hobnobbing with the in crowd at the hotel was a joy. Jolson continued to go to the pool early every morning and belt out songs like "Red, Red Robin." Instead of finding it objectionable, Joe began to wax sentimental when "Jolie" would pour on the schmaltz with lines like "live, love, laugh, and be happy."

Joe even went in for golf, making up a crazy foursome: Lou Costello, Bill Smith, Al Ritz, and Joe Frisco. His first shot was a complete miss. "T-T-Tennis is my racket," he cracked. It certainly wasn't golf. On each green, Costello would divert Joe's attention, while Ritz replaced Joe's ball with a ringer. Frisco would then putt for the cup and the trick ball would roll cockeyed. Joe never tumbled that he was being taken until, on the last tee, he hit and exploded a loaded ball, which went off with a bang!

Good-natured fun was the order of the day. These were memorable weeks. Then, as Jack Pepper tells it, a strange man came looking for Joe Frisco. Joe had gone over to Desert Hot Springs with Jolson for the mineral baths. Pepper, who has a way of ingratiating himself with everyone, learned that this man was from the Internal Revenue Service. Joe Frisco had never paid taxes in his life, though in his time he had opened some pretty hefty pay envelopes. He owed the government enough money to buy a stable of thoroughbred racehorses.

Each year Joe would return the income tax form and scribble across it the three words he could write: "Got no money." Uncle Sam finally caught up with him when the phrase "Got no money" was for real. Joe's salary now was only five hundred a week. There was a time when he had paid that much to his agent in commissions. Along with the thousands of dollars he owed in back taxes, the fines and penalties pyramided the total to an astronomical figure. After a stormy hearing and a herculean assist from a nationally famous politician, a deal was made. It was agreed that the management of the Chi-Chi Club would retain and turn over to the Collector of Internal Revenue $150 each week from Joe Frisco's salary. Furthermore, the management firmed the deal by guaranteeing Frisco's employment for the entire Palm Springs season.

As Frisco and his entourage left the federal building, Joe was the only member who felt he was abused. "Boy," he complained, "if I ever get even, I'll never do b-b-business with that firm again."

13

Charlie's "Sucker" Club

At this time Charlie Foy was running his own supper club out in the San Fernando Valley. One night after the Palm Springs season was over, Joe Frisco drifted in to visit with Charlie, who offered him work. Joe said he wasn't interested in working for the tax man. He was bitter about Uncle Sam tapping his pay envelope every week. He called it blackmail. When Charlie Foy coaxed him out on the floor, Joe turned his pockets inside out. He said, "In case there's an Internal Revenue man here tonight, I just want him to know that I'm broke."

"How come you're broke tonight?" quizzed Charlie. "I heard you had a hundred dollars on you this morning."

"I did, b-b-but I went to the track," replied Joe.

"The track," laughed Charlie. "The track wasn't open today."

"I found that out," retorted Joe, "so I tore up the money."

Joe delighted the patrons of the Club. He'd say a simple line like, "Welcome to the Foy Sucker Club," and the Hollywood crowd would fall in the aisle laughing at him. In spite of this, Charlie Foy couldn't induce him to work there—at least not steadily.

"Why should I work for de duck?" he kept asking.

"What in the hell is de duck?" asked Foy.

"The t-t-tax man. Every week I would work, he'd de duck a hundred and fifty bucks."

"If they tap your paycheck here, I'll go fifty-fifty with you," Charlie assured him.

Joe shook hands and said, "You got a deal, b-b-but one more thing. I saw a man buy a drink at the bar for fifty cents. You gotta get a buck a drink or no Frisco."

Charlie was furious at Joe's ultimatum, but he agreed to experiment. "I'll try the new price for one week," he promised. Joe's suggestion was good. The take doubled and continued to mount. The motion picture crowd came in droves, and none was too big to become a stooge for Joe Frisco. After his act, he'd wander through the audience with a portable microphone, sometimes telling gags and sometimes coaxing the customers to sing. One night in an attempt to rib Bing Crosby, he pushed the mike into the hand of a man sitting ringside. "Mister," he said, "Bing Crosby sang in this microphone not too long ago, and today he's a s-s-star. If he can make it, anyone can."

The man took the mike and stood up. To the orchestra leader he said, "One Enchanted Evening, in B-flat please." Joe did a take and then did an "Off to Buffalo" from the scene. The man sang in a voice that would have made Ezio Pinza hide under a table. He was on his third encore when Joe rushed to Charlie Foy. "Quick," he said, "g-g-grab this guy. S-s-sign him up; he's dynamite."

"Joe," said Charlie impatiently, "that man's name is Lawrence Tibbett."

"So what," shouted Joe. "You can ch-ch-change his name."

Foy had an apartment over the club. He had twin beds, so Frisco moved in. The very first night they sat and gabbed for hours. The subject? Horses, of course.

At six A.M. Charlie was startled. Almost in perfect rhythm Joe was groaning—"Oh—oh—ouch—ugh—ooh—gee."

Charlie jumped up and shook the sleeping Frisco. In a stupor Joe sat up, felt the back of his head, and obviously was relieved to find he wasn't bleeding and had no lumps.

"Oh, what a nightmare," he gasped, "I dreamt I made a bet on a hurdle race. It turned out my b-b-bed was one of the hurdles and as each horse cleared, its rear hoof k-k-kicked me in the head."

"Now I know why people say you're horse crazy," said Foy.

A few days later Joe picked up a stray cat. Obviously it wasn't housebroken. Foy came home late. The smell was god-awful. He shook Joe. "You've had that stinkin' cat in here again." Before Frisco could answer, Charlie spotted a whole mountain of deposit on the floor. "There it is," Foy screamed. "The whole place stinks. I'm going out of here for a half hour. If that mess isn't cleaned up before I get back, so help me, I'll burn down the goddamn building with you in it," and he stomped out of his own apartment.

When he returned, he saw Frisco had washed the spot on the rug. Now Charlie undressed, put on his pajamas, and crawled into bed. As soon as he laid his head on the pillow the smell was worse than before. He jumped up and shook Joe and yelled, "I said clean up that stinkin' cat dirt."

"I did clean it up," Joe yelled back. Then pointing between the twin beds, he continued, "If you think I'm lying, I'll prove it to you. Just look in that w-w-wastebasket."

That did it. Charlie got so provoked, he got dressed and announced dramatically, "I'm checking into a motel tonight and you're paying for it." He walked out and slammed the door. The Los Angeles area was having a torrential rain, and at every motel, Charlie found a "no vacancy" sign. Meanwhile, Frisco, who was a terrible coward, locked and bolted the door. He also pushed the dresser and a couple of chairs against it. He then curled up and buried his head under the covers. Reluctantly, Charlie came home. He put his key in the door only to find the inside bolt was engaged. The porch had no roof, so Charlie was standing in the driving rain. He pounded and pounded on the door. Finally, he got a weak "Who is it?"

"It's me, Charlie, hurry up and open the door."

Came the reply, "Foy's not here."

"This is Foy," came back the wet wail. "For God's sake let me in."

From behind the door came the scared, quaking voice of Joe Frisco, talking fast. "You're not Foy, you're not Charlie Foy. Foy said he wasn't coming home tonight. I got a gun, get away from the d-d-door or I'll shoot."

There was thunder and lightning, and the rain was just pouring down. Now Foy started to panic because he actually kept a loaded gun in the room.

"Joe, Joe," he pleaded, "don't you recognize my voice?"

"I'll shoot, so help me. G-g-get away, I'll shoot."

Charlie was actually sobbing now. "It's me, Joe, honest to God. I couldn't get a room. Let me in before I get pneumonia."

"If you're really Charlie," came the quivering reply, "let me hear you sing your opening number."

Charlie's opening number was as long as the opera *La Bohème*. There he stood on his own porch at three o'clock in the morning in a furious downpour, forced to sing to prove that he was Charlie Foy so that he could get into his own apartment. Sing he did, and he did it as if he were in the Hollywood Bowl.

"I'm just one of a great family from New Rochelle.
I'm the son of a famous father, you all knew him well.
All year long we travel, we go home to rest in June.
There's no rest for the rest of us on a Sunday afternoon."

Now Charlie stopped singing. "You recognized that, didn't ya, Joe?"

He got a two-word answer: "Finish it!"

By now Foy was wilting, but he picked up where he left off and sang another sixteen bars. Then again he started pleading.

"Joe, please open the goddamn door. What the hell do you think I am—a duck?"

"Finish that opening number," demanded Joe.

"I did finish it," an exasperated Charlie insisted.

"Well, sing it again," directed Frisco, "because I like your voice better without music."

The following day Charlie Foy spent most of his time walking around kicking cats. Joe Frisco covered ten miles in the bedroom pacing and pouting. The Damon and Pythias of the nightclubs refused to talk to each other. When show time arrived, Foy opened, as usual, singing the now weatherbeaten song, but he fluffed the lyrics twice and actually sang the damn song worse than he had the previous night on the porch in the thunderstorm.

Cully Richards came next. Cully was ever popular with the nightclub audiences. He clowned a bit, gathered a few yocks, and then brought on Margaret Whiting, who conked the audience with the surefire melodies of her father's hit songs. Now came a sketch with Joe Frisco, Cully Richards, and Charlie's sister, Mary Foy. Fortunately, it was in pantomime. Cully faced the audience dressed as a minister. Joe and Mary were facing the minister with their backs to the audience. They were dressed as bride and groom. The preacher went through the motions of blessing them. Joe placed the ring on Mary's finger. Then in pantomime Cully conveyed, "I now pronounce you man and wife." The band played the Wedding March, and as Mary and Joe turned to face the audience for the first time, it saw Mary with a pillow in her dress, stuffed out in front like she was ten months pregnant. The audience howled.

It was now Joe's turn to do his stint. Usually, he started by greeting individuals in the audience and generally improvised little quips about them. On this night, he just couldn't get started. He not only stuttered but also mumbled and muttered.

In the audience was a self-important actor who had clicked in a few pictures and with each degree of success had gotten a little bit more obnoxious.

"Hey, Joe," he heckled, "take the marbles out of your mouth."

"They're not marbles," bounced back Joe, "they're radishes, and to p-p-prove it, I'll ad-lib a big belch—just for you." And he did.

The audience enjoyed the squelch as well as the belch and applauded. This was just the lift that Joe needed, but suddenly there was a stir in the audience and an excitement that became audible. This was the night of the Academy Awards, the year that the talented Bette Davis won the coveted Oscar as best actress. After a night of intense excitement, she had decided it might be relaxing to stop off at the Foy Supper Club, where she could let her hair down and have a few laughs.

The maître d' sat Miss Davis at a ringside table, and as the audience gradually recognized her, pandemonium broke out. Joe stopped trying to talk and held up his hand for quiet. "P-P-Please," he pleaded and eventually a hush came over the place. Nervous as a frightened pup, Joe went into a flowery introduction. He really outdid himself. Never before had Joe been so eloquent or articulate. Finally, he wound up—"S-S-So now, ladies and gentlemen, I give you Miss Bette Hutton."

Though unintended, this boo-boo got a belly laugh. Even Bette Davis laughed; but after the applause subsided, she turned to Frisco and said, "Thank you, Joe Palooka."

After the show that night, Foy got a call for him and for Frisco. A racetrack pal had been stricken at Hollywood and Vine with a heart attack and had been rushed to the Georgia Street Receiving Hospital. This guy, whom they knew only as Max, was a real character. He knew all the jockeys and horse trainers and on numerous occasions had given the boys some good information. Invariably, this man would tout himself off his own tip and switch to the wrong horse. Max was a born loser; he was never in the money.

At two A.M., Charlie and Joe drove to Georgia Street Receiving Hospital. They knew Max was penniless, and to the best of their knowledge he had no kin, so they felt obligated to make sure he was being cared for. The floor nurse broke all the rules. She walked them through several wards until they spotted Max. He was in a coma and looked ghastly. Charlie immediately fell to his knees and started praying. Joe took a second look at Max and said, "Good God, when I was a kid, we used to make better looking f-f-faces on a s-s-snowman."

The nurse read the chart and informed the boys that there was little chance of the patient lasting through the night. Charlie thanked the nurse for being so considerate, and Joe said, "N-N-Nurse, if he happens to p-p-pull through, t-t-tell him we were asking for him."

Max didn't pull through. The next morning Joe learned that the body had been sent to the city morgue. Hoping to arrange for a decent burial, Frisco went to the morgue and again went through the routine of identifying Max.

"There are three bodies in this room and another half a dozen downstairs," informed the attendant, who then walked over to a slab and said, "Here is number one." "Nope, n-n-not him," said Joe. The attendant walked a few steps to the right, pointed, and said, "Here's number two." Joe shook his head negatively. "Well," continued the attendant, "here's the third one." "No, that's not him either," to which Joe added, "Poor Max, he's out of the money again." He found Max's body downstairs.

Joe decided not to tell Foy, but he was determined to keep Max's body out of the potter's field. He went back to the Club and, immediately upon entering the room, said, "Foy, I have to have three hundred dollars right away."

"You gotta be crazy," said Charlie. "You know I just made a big payoff on this place and I need a hundred right now myself. If I don't raise a couple hundred we'll have no liquor to sell for the weekend." Charlie didn't like the expression on Joe's face, so he decided to try to soften him up. He dug into his pants pocket, pulled out his money, and said, "Will fifty help you until Monday?"

Joe was adamant. "I said three hundred. With the business we're doing, if you can't d-d-dig up three hundred for me, you b-b-better dig up a new b-b-boy for tonight."

Charlie succumbed to the pressure. "C'mon, we'll go to Hollywood.

There's a certain guy helped me out a couple of times; but I'm pressing my luck. He thinks I'm too careless with a buck. Says I gotta stop throwing my money around."

"You sure throw it," Joe sneered, "from one p-p-pocket to the other."

They got into the car. It was a sunny day. Charlie asked Joe to hand him his sunglasses from the glove compartment. When Frisco reached into the compartment, he happened to notice the pink slip from the Department of Motor Vehicles.

"You own this car outright, don't you, Charlie?"

"Certainly," was the reply. "I paid cash for it."

They drove about a mile east on Ventura Boulevard, and suddenly Joe asked Charlie to pull into the Bank of America parking lot.

"Just sit here a few minutes," Joe suggested. "I wanna see a guy inside."

Through the bank window Charlie watched Joe Frisco. He was seated at a big desk, earnestly conversing with a man who appeared to be a bank executive. The man opened a drawer and pulled out some papers, and immediately Joe started signing them. Soon a younger man came to the desk, and it appeared that the executive and Joe were both giving him instructions. Then the chap, carrying a clipboard and pencil, walked to the car.

"Mr. Foy?" he inquired.

"Yes, I'm Mr. Foy," was the reply.

"Well, sir, you are wanted in the bank."

As Charlie walked toward the entrance, he turned and noticed that the young man lifted the hood of his car and wrote down the motor number. Confused and nervous, he hurried into the bank.

"What's up, Joe?"

Frisco was real smug. "Charlie, this is Mr. Ramsfelder. He's taking g-g-good care of me. Just sign this p-p-paper here."

"What is it for?" asked Charlie.

"The money, Foy, the money. We don't have to go to Hollywood for it—we're g-g-getting it right here. Five hundred dollars. Three for me and the t-t-two you need to b-b-buy the liquor for the Club. Just sign the paper."

Not until then did Charlie Foy realize that Joe Frisco had just hocked the Foy automobile.

The next morning was a very busy one for Joe Frisco. He had to attend to two very important functions, the burial of Max and the opening day of Hollywood Park Racetrack. Joe went to the office of a famous mortician. He couldn't have been more dramatically impressive if he had put raw onions in his handkerchief to make his eyes water. The mortician was very cooperative.

"Mr. Frisco, did I understand you to say that the man had no kin, and that you don't know his full name or his faith?"

"We only knew him as M-M-Max."

"Then why have a costly burial, Mr. Frisco? We will arrange to pick up Max's body and arrange for the cremation. We will have a fine, dignified, nonsectarian service and place his ashes under a rosebush in our own private cemetery. Mr. Frisco, we will do all of this for one hundred dollars."

Suddenly realizing he would end up with two hundred dollars in his pocket for the opening of Hollywood Park, Joe in his most solemn manner said, "Thank you sir, this is just the way M-M-Max would have wanted it."

Joe signed the necessary papers releasing Max's body. He then gave the mortician one hundred dollars, for which he received his receipt. To look at Joe's expression as he walked to his car, one never would have believed he had just left a funeral parlor. He looked like he had just won a three-horse parlay. By noon Joe arrived at the racetrack. Foy had been waiting for him. He had arranged for two seats at a table that sat four. With apologies, Goldie, the maître d', explained that because of the unprecedented crowd for this opening day, they would have to share a table with a couple. As they walked toward their places, Charlie spotted the couple, and he whispered, "Get a load of that broad; she looks like Harpo Marx."

"Harpo is p-p-prettier," added Joe.

"It's gonna be a rough day for me," Charlie complained. "Get a load of the cigar that guy is puffing on."

"Hm," topped Joe, "I thought he was eating a banana—I just hope he d-d-doesn't exhale."

By this time they had reached the table, which was already covered with newspapers, scratch sheets, the *Racing Form,* and three different colored pencils. There was enough paraphernalia to last the average horseplayer a season. The boys nodded and sat down. Suddenly Joe started to squirm; then he turned green. Wherever he looked on the table he saw ashes. The tray, the saucer, even the top of the tip sheet—everywhere he saw ashes. "Oh God," he moaned, "Max's remains are coming back to haunt me."

Just before the first race, the man behind the cigar, after acting like a human calculating machine, laid down his pencil and said, "Boys, I don't know whether you're aware of it, but the most important thing about picking winning racehorses is figures. Figures tell the whole story. Figures don't lie."

After the first race Joe proudly displayed the winning ticket. Came the second race and Joe got lucky again, but when he also caught the winner in the third, Frisco got real cocky. He licked the back of the winning ticket and stuck it on his forehead for Mr. Ashes to see.

"You're remarkable," said the stranger. "I'd certainly like to know how you made your choices. I've been playing horses all my life. I have all kinds of statistics, and that's how I come by my figures. When you doubt figures, you can't play the horses. How do you do it?"

"Well, I'll tell you how I came to play those horses," said Frisco. "When the horses come out on the t-t-track, I look to see which ones are nervous. See that number one horse? Notice how nervous he is. That horse is fractious. He's dying to g-g-go. Now you see the number eight horse out there? He's behaving the same way. He's anxious and just dying to go, too."

"Right," said the bewildered stranger, "but how do you pick the winner?"

"Well, er, I take one from eight," explained Joe cautiously, "and then I b-b-bet on number six."

"But," persisted the man, "one from eight is seven."

To which Frisco replied, "There you go with your g-g-goddamn figures again."

Before the fourth race the boys decided on a change of atmosphere. They walked over to George Raft's box. No one attracted more friends or more touts than George Raft. Al Ritz, the elder of the Ritz brothers, whispered, "Play number seven, guys. I got it from Johnny Longden's wife." Al Ritz's wife says, "I wish my husband would listen to his own wife for a change; number four can't lose." Maxie Rosenbloom pipes up, "You're all nuts. Number six will waltz in."

All this chatter confused Frisco. He asked Foy for change for a twenty. Charlie handed him two tens, but Joe was so nervous, he took the tens and handed the twenty not to Charlie but to Rosenbloom; and Maxie was so nervous, he kept it!

Seated close to Raft was MGM exec Al Lichtman, who had Nick the Greek as his guest. Nick's lips were sealed. His tips were never revealed, unless you followed Al to the hundred-dollar window and caught a glimpse as the clerk punched out twenty or thirty tickets. Rose Lichtman, Al's wife, always lingered in front of the two-dollar window. As Frisco approached, she asked, "Who's gonna win, Joe?"

"Number nine—it c-c-can't lose," was the reply.

She glanced at her program—"Oh good, a long shot"—and immediately she bought a two-dollar ticket on number nine.

A mile and a sixteenth—they're off—Lichtman's horse is out front flying—number nine, in the rear, dying. At the half mile, it's a one-horse race. Suddenly nine's moving up on the pace. At the quarter pole, of all things, number nine is taking on wings—and wins. What an upset!

"I win, I win," shouted Rose. And win she did. She won twenty-eight dollars, while Al, following Nick's tip, lost three thousand. Proudly she waved the two-dollar ticket in Al's face. "See? See?" she kept screeching excitedly.

Al was so infuriated, he kicked her where she usually sits. Rose didn't even feel it. Ignoring her husband's fury, she ran to see Frisco. "Joe," she shouted, "gee, thanks. I hope you had a bundle on number nine."

"I didn't bet number nine," Joe confessed.

"How come?" asked Rose. "You told me it couldn't lose."

"I know," agreed Frisco, "but I'm such a liar."

Business at Foy's Club always boomed when the Hollywood Park track opened. Most of the people who frequented the races knew Joe Frisco or knew of him and knew at least several of his famous racetrack stories. In fact, Joe's most popular comedy routine was "The Horse Room." It was hilariously funny to anyone who had ever experienced the nervous tension that permeates a betting room during and between the calling of the races. The character Joe played was really an imitation of himself: an addicted horseplayer with a cigar in his mouth, a pencil behind his ear, a rumpled *Racing Form* under one arm, and a newspaper under the other. In his hand he held a scratch sheet, and sticking out of his pocket was the green sheet. Between arguments and discussions with other, imaginary bettors, there was utter confusion. While trying to weigh the opinion of one handicapper against that of another, he would switch from one paper to the sheet and then back to the other newspaper. Finally, while holding the *Racing Form* between his knees, he would try to spread out the newspaper and mark it with his cigar, while he puffed away madly on the pencil.

Jockeys Pierson, Eddie Arcaro, Jackie Westrope, and Nick Wall were all frequent visitors to the club. They all thought Joe was so excruciatingly funny that they could laugh even while paying their checks.

Knowing a jockey certainly doesn't guarantee a win at a racetrack. On one occasion, however, Joe had information right from the horse's mouth. It happened the day before a hundred-thousand-dollar race. Every handicapper in every paper picked the famous thoroughbred Mioland as the odds-on favorite. The jockey, Jackie Westrope, was confident that he had no competition. It was a big, important race. The purse was $103,900. The winner got $89,360.

On Friday afternoon, jockey Nick Wall, casually looking up at the sky, said to Joe Frisco, "Looks a bit cloudy. If we could get a lot of rain tonight, I can upset the applecart in the big race tomorrow."

Joe laughingly said, "I'll have Foy g-g-go to church for ya and say a prayer. God never listens to me."

Nick was scheduled to ride Bay View, the longest shot in the race. Not a single handicapper gave this horse a smell or a lick. All Nick added was, "Bay View loves the mud."

On the way home from the track, it started to drizzle, but Joe forgot even to mention to Foy his conversation with Nick. At the club that night, when it was time to do his second show, Joe peeked out at the empty room and said, "Where the hell is everybody? I left more people at home in my b-b-bed." The downpour killed business. Too many streets were flooded. The show that night was more like a dress rehearsal.

When they went to bed the rain was still falling, and in the morning when Joe looked out the window the view was like you'd get from a houseboat. "No track today," commented Foy, "a guy would have to be nuts to brave this weather."

Suddenly Joe recalled his conversation with Nicky Wall and relayed it to Charlie. "Nick says this horse Bay View loves mud."

Charlie grabbed the phone and dialed Connie Hurley, a popular bookmaker. "Hello, Connie, this is Foy, what's the price on Bay View in the big race? Fifty? Fifty to one! Er, lemme ask ya, do you pay track odds? What? Fifteen, six, and three. Oh, thanks." Charlie hung up, turned to Joe, and said, "C'mon, get dressed, it's gonna be tough goin', but we're headin' for the track."

The fourth race was just finishing when they arrived. They had no seats, so they donned their raincoats and went down to the rail by the finish line. They saw two races, and then came the hundred grander.

Joe bet twenty on Bay View's nose, and Charlie bet five across the board. The nervous tension was mounting. When the bugler came out before the race and played the familiar fanfare, Joe sighed contentedly. "Ah," he said, "there's music. Irving Berlin never wrote a melody as pretty as that."

They're off and running! Bay View flies out of the gate. He's out in front and he stays out there all around the track. Westrope is riding Mioland, the big favorite, and just as they reach the wire he comes on with a rush. A hush comes over the park. No one knows who won. It was a photo finish. It seems like hours. Then finally the tote board lights up and, lo and behold, number eight is the winner. Nicky Wall's mount Bay View did it! Cheers and boos—and then the price is flashed on the board. He paid $118.40 to win. Wow!

Joe Frisco was shaking. Charlie gave him a whooping slap on the back, but Joe didn't notice. He was spellbound.

"C'mon Joe, let's get going and beat this crowd. Get over and get your money. You got over eleven hundred bucks coming."

"Charlie," said Joe weakly, "d-d-do me a favor. I can't move—take my ticket and g-g-go cash it."

"No," shouted Charlie, "cash your own ticket. I've got a five-dollar combination of my own, and I'd have to go to two windows. We'll never get home. Go cash your own ticket."

"I c-c-can't, Charlie; please, I c-c-can't move."

"What's the matter, Joe, what happened?"

Meekly came the reply, "S-S-Someone shit in my p-p-pants."

After a win like that, a man generally leaves the track smelling like a rose, but as Charlie said in the car while driving home, "There's only one Joe Frisco"—to which he added, "Thank God."

14

The Joker Is Wild

Every tourist who ever visited Hollywood has seen Grauman's Chinese Theatre. Sid Grauman created the idea of preserving the footprints of movie stars in cement, in the forecourt of his Hollywood Boulevard theatre. Sid was also famous for being a practical joker, and he got an extra bang out of ribbing Joe Frisco. On the Saturday night that Bay View won the big race, Grauman phoned Joe and said, "Sorry I didn't see you at the track today. I had to stay here and attend to business. Our company had a very special meeting, and I want you to know your name was the main topic of conversation. I suddenly came to the realization," Sid went on, "that my friend Joe Frisco, the most popular comic among the people of our industry, is not represented in my theatre. I have Fred Astaire's footprints and also Gene Kelly's. I have John Barrymore's profile, and I even have Jolson's knee- and handprints."

Joe interrupted eagerly, "You mean I'm g-g-gonna get my footprints in the forecourt of the Chinese Theatre?"

"Not footprints, Joe," said Grauman. "After the demonstration you gave in front of fifty thousand people at the race today, we decided you should *sit down* in the cement."

"Well," Joe stuttered, "Moses went into the promised land on his ass, so mine should be good enough for Grauman's Chinese."

Joe didn't take this ribbing "sitting down." He slammed the phone on the hook, leapt to his feet, and went looking for Foy. He found Charlie in the kitchen having a bowl of soup.

"There you are, Mr. b-b-big mouth. Didja have to tell Sid Grauman I did my business in my pants? Dirty d-d-double-crosser."

Charlie laughed so hard he sprayed onion soup all over his suit and necktie, and when he finally got through coughing and getting the soup out of his windpipe, he said, "Joe, you're nuts, I haven't told a soul what happened to you."

"Then how did Sid Grauman know that I sh-sh-er had an accident?"

"Ya walked to the parking lot, didn't ya?"

"What's that got to d-d-do with it?"

"Well, Mr. Frisco, any friends who know you didn't just have a prostate operation and saw you walk had to know that you had a load of something in your pants."

"You're a lousy s-s-stinker and you know it," shouted Joe, and then, infuriated, he pushed the swinging door with such force that the rebound knocked him sprawling.

Early the next morning the phone rang. Disturbed, Foy groaned, "Who the hell calls people at eight in the morning?"

"I bet it's Grauman with his d-d-damn ribbing," said Joe. "Well, he's not gonna get me again." With that, Joe pulled the covers over his head and curled up.

Charlie answered the phone. It was Western Union with a night letter for Joe Frisco. The operator read a lengthy message to Charlie from Joe's sister, Mae. Joe's mother had died in her sleep, and Mae was pleading for Joe to come to Dubuque. She needed his help. Charlie pondered for a moment and then gently tapped the little guy on the shoulder. "Joe, wake up."

"Go 'way, Foy. Today is Sunday; g-g-go to church and say your prayers and I'll see ya when you get back. I'm sleepy."

"Joe, wake up. I have sad news for you," Charlie gently explained.

"Sad news," laughed Frisco. "What'd they do, put up an inquiry sign on yesterday's race?"

"Frisco, this is no time for clowning. You just got a telegram from your sister, Mae, that's gonna make you very sad."

Startled, Joe snapped out of it. He swung around quickly and sat up in bed. "What'sa matter, what happened?" he asked anxiously. "What is it?"

"Joe," said Charlie sadly, "it's your mother; she died. She just went to sleep, pal. Your mom is out of her misery at long last."

Frisco sat there, stunned. "Oh, Jesus," he exclaimed, "I couldn't even be there to comfort her at the end."

"Now, don't berate yourself," said Charlie. "She's in God's hands now, but your sister needs your help."

"I'll send her some money right away," said Joe.

"You will not send—you'll take!" reprimanded Charlie.

"No! Oh no, Charlie, I am not going. I don't wanna see my mother in a wooden box. I'm not going, I wanna remember her like she was."

"Joe," persisted Charlie, in a fatherly tone. "Your sister needs more than just money. She needs your help to make decisions. There is no family burial plot, and because of the shortage of money she thought possibly your mom should be cremated."

"Cremated!" screamed Joe. "Cremated? God," and now he sobbed hysterically. "Cremated! My mother? My sister, Mae, must be crazy—out of her m-m-mind. That's my mom, not some, er, some unloved racetrack character—er—like Max."

"Now calm down, Joe, your sister will abide by your wishes. That's why she wants you there."

Charlie, who gave a spiritual equation to everything that happened in the world, said: "The good Lord has a way of making things fall into their proper place. Thanks to fate, you have over twelve hundred dollars in your pocket. You can fly home today and get there in time to arrange a fine funeral for your mom. Just the way you want it. Now get up, take a shower, and get dressed. I'll phone the airport and get you out on the first plane."

"Oh, Charlie, you sweet son of a bitch," he sobbed. "What would I ever do without you?"

As a relief from grief, many people go to the Bible and get consolation from prayers. Joe didn't know how to pray. Charlie Foy always did it for him.

Immediately after Joe's mother was put to rest, his skin got too tight for his bones. He had to run—somewhere—anywhere. He chose Chicago; then he hopped a plane for Los Angeles. But before boarding, he rushed to the newsstand. He still could not read but was quite proficient at decoding a *Racing Form*. For the second time in a week he was going from a funeral to the racetrack. He was sad, grief stricken, and depressed, but as soon as the plane took off, he buried his face in the *Racing Form*. It was like a catharsis—all the sorrow of the past few days vanished.

It seemed like only ten minutes had passed when they announced Los Angeles International Airport. On arrival, Joe took inventory. He had thirteen dollars. He found a bus that took him to a point in Inglewood where he could change to another bus that took him right to Hollywood Park. The horses were on the track. He didn't even take time out to look for Charlie. Five minutes after he got off the bus he had already made his first bet. The fifth race was over when he ran into Crosby. "How ya doing?" inquired Bing.

"I just tapped out," said Joe, "b-b-but my luck's not all bad or I wouldn't have b-b-bumped into you."

Bing smiled, dug into his pockets, peeled off his roll. "Here's a double sawbuck, puss, and with it goes a bit of advice: throw away your *Racing Form* and bet this twenty on number two. Don't let the price scare you; it might get you well."

Der Bingle was sent from Heaven. As the horses stormed out of the starting gate, number two was nowhere. He trailed for half a mile, then he started moving up steadily. In the stretch, he forged ahead gamely and won by three-quarters of a length. Joe collected $238.

That was all it took. Joe floated right to the bar. "Set 'em up, Freddie," he shouted. "The drinks are on me." With this kind of an announcement, you can always draw an audience. Soon Joe was surrounded. He was really buoyant. He bounced a few wisecracks off the bartender, and then with about eight guys around him he said, "Gee, I have as big an audience here as we g-g-get some nights at the Foy Supper Club." Immediately, he took on the assignment of raconteur, entertaining the freeloaders. Even the losers were laughing loudly, when in walked Crosby.

"Hello, Lucky," shouted the groaner. "Remember me?"

Joe paused long enough to pull out his newly acquired bankroll and peel a twenty-dollar bill off the top.

"C'mere, boy," he said, waving the twenty in Bing's direction. "This is for you." He handed Bing the bill, tapped him on the back, and said, "Now, son, how about a c-c-couple of choruses of 'M-M-Melancholy Baby'?"

Charlie wasn't at the track that day. He had to attend to some business and hadn't the slightest notion that Joe had returned home. Crosby drove Joe to town and dropped him at Hollywood and Vine. With a couple of hundred dollars still in his pocket, Joe headed for the Brown Derby. It was eleven P.M. when Joe finally reached Foy's Supper Club feeling no pain. He greeted Charlie with the enthusiasm of a twelve-year-old who had just returned from his first visit to Disneyland.

"When the hell did you get back?" inquired a very offended Foy.

Cully Richards, who was on the floor performing when Frisco walked in, cut his routine abruptly and enthusiastically announced, "Ladies and gentlemen, the prodigal son has returned. It's an ill wind that blows no one good. The bookmakers will light candles tonight. With a big hand, folks, welcome back the one and only Joe Frisco." Joe walked out onto the floor and received an ovation. He went right to work and never was better. Charlie Foy was elated over Joe's success. During Joe's absence Charlie had been through a very dull week.

Cowboy star Gene Autry enjoyed Frisco so much that night he offered him a small part in a picture. He really didn't need Joe, but he was excited and wanted to get him on the set. He honestly thought it might lead to something better.

"It's just a quick shot," drawled Autry. "You're supposed to be a country dentist. We're riding in a stagecoach together. My face is swollen and I've got a toothache and you're called upon to pull my tooth."

Frisco looked askance. "I gotta pull your tooth?"

"What's the matter, Joe, are you squeamish?"

"What does it pay?" inquired Joe.

"Oh," replied Autry, "a hundred dollars."

"A hundred dollars," repeated Joe, disgusted. "One hundred bucks! My dentist gets more than that, and he isn't even in s-s-show business."

Autry felt a bit crushed, but agent Joe Glaser, visiting from Chicago, heard the conversation. "Joe Frisco," he explained to Autry, "would never bend when it came to making terms for a job." Glaser said that once when Joe was six weeks in arrears at the Hotel Sherman, he called and offered Joe a week's work at $1,000.

"My salary is f-f-fifteen hundred," replied Joe.

"An hour later," Glaser said, "I phoned again to say I had succeeded in upping the offer to $1,250."

"No d-d-dice," Joe replied, "my salary is $1,500."

"There was more fruitless talk, till I said, 'Joe, I expect the man here within a half hour. Maybe between us we can convince him to make it fifteen, so get off your butt and get over here to my office right now.'"

"What," bellowed Joe, "and get locked out of my hotel room?"

Business progressed swimmingly at the club. Joe's popularity grew in leaps and bounds. He brought in enough money for the club to prosper.

The relationship between Foy and Frisco was beautiful. They had great affection for one another, in spite of the fact that neither of the two guys sang soprano. Charlie, younger than Joe, acted more like the father. In fact, Joe, always a Peck's Bad Boy, needed several fathers.

One night Charlie flew down to San Diego, came home at eight A.M., and saw flames shooting out of his apartment over the Club. The fire department immediately answered the call; fortunately the damage was minor. Seeing Frisco in his pajamas, a fireman turned to him and said, "It's your good fortune we got here as soon as we did."

A second fireman said to Joe, "You're lucky to be alive; I guess this will teach you not to smoke in bed."

"I didn't smoke in bed," declared Frisco, indignantly.

"Then who started the fire?" asked the chief.

"I don't know," stammered Frisco, "it was b-b-burning when I went to bed."

Charlie Foy never did figure out how the fire got started.

When Thanksgiving arrived, Charlie found himself in a real dilemma. Each Thanksgiving he gave a turkey dinner for the staff and their families. The chef made the turkey and set it aside to cool before carving. Twenty-four diners arrived and were sitting at a huge table enjoying relish and appetizers. Suddenly it was discovered that the turkey had vanished, just plain disappeared. Embarrassed and frantic, Charlie enlisted the aid of everyone short of J. Edgar Hoover. Confused and in utter despair, he quizzed all the people who worked in the building.

"Look," he announced, "the bird had already been roasted, so it couldn't fly away. Now, I want to know who—" Just then Joe Frisco stuck his head through the doorway. "What do you want, Frisco?" asked Charlie. "Do you know who got away with our Thanksgiving dinner?"

"D-d-don't look at me with an accusing eye," stuttered Joe. "If you think I ate your goddamn t-t-turkey—weigh me!"

Republic Pictures was shooting a musical called *Atlantic City*. When it was nearing completion, the powers that be thought it needed help. There was a nightclub scene, and the producer sold the organization on adding Joe Frisco to do two specialties. Joe had long since decided against any attempt at becoming a moving picture actor; however, the idea of just doing a specialty appealed to him.

He was offered four thousand dollars for two days' work: his classic bit, "The Man in the Horse Room," and a revival of his famous jazz dance. The dance they planned to stage just as Ziegfeld had done it. They guaranteed to shoot the two scenes within thirty days after signing contracts. Republic's publicists went right to work. Joe Frisco was good copy. As one columnist put it, "The guy's humor is priceless. He has a built-in gag file in his head."

Tom Duggan's TV show was popular then, and he was a big Frisco fan. He'd get Joe on the air and engage in horseracing talk. The patter between them went something like this:

"You still go to the track every day, Joe?"

"Yeah, but I'm taking a cure to b-b-break the habit."

"You take medicine? You got a doctor?"

"No, no medicine. He ain't that kind of a d-d-doctor."

"Is he a psychiatrist?"

"No, he's a Hungarian feller—little guy."

"Where's his office?"

"Just down the street, about s-s-six furlongs."

"You couldn't mean a mile and an eighth?"

"No, this doctor's old, I don't think he could g-g-go that distance."

This kind of patter went on endlessly. Duggan was equally fond of Foy and the whole Foy family. He had them on his show often, which boosted attendance for the Charlie Foy Supper Club. Charlie was delighted over the additional revenue that Joe was drawing into the club, and to show his appreciation he let him take Sunday off. Joe had a yen to go to Tijuana for the Sunday races. With Hollywood Park closed, a day at Caliente had the same satisfying effect on Joe as a shot in the arm to a drug addict. On that Sunday afternoon, Charlie got a long-distance call from Cleveland that was intended for Frisco. It came from a woman who said she was a friend of Loretta McDermott. The call obviously came from a phone booth, and after three minutes' conversation, it was over.

Foy insisted it was Loretta, drunk as a hoot owl and trying to disguise her voice. The story in brief was that she and Eddie Cox had split and that she was sick and destitute. She had no one left to turn to and felt sure Joe would help her through this crisis. Charlie never had any use for Loretta, and he took it on himself to give her a verbal spanking. Reluctantly, however, he promised to deliver her message. The party said she was phoning from the depot but could be reached the next day at the Hotel Grant in Chicago. Foy's account of the phone call was more like a tirade than a message, and it didn't strike a very responsive note with Joe. His deep-rooted concern for Loretta manifested itself instantly. Charlie had never seen Joe display such violent temper. He snarled at Foy and told him in no uncertain terms to mind his own goddamn business.

Next day, when Joe couldn't make any contact with Loretta, he carried on like a madman. She was not registered at the Grant Hotel, nor did she have a reservation.

"Don't worry," fumed Charlie, "you'll hear from her as soon as she sobers up. Where else could she find a soft touch like Joe Frisco? He's never let her down in the past."

Thank heavens, at that moment the phone rang—or Joe surely would have committed mayhem. Instead, he grabbed the receiver, thinking it might be her. It was Republic Pictures. Shooting was to commence on Wednesday morning at eight o'clock.

"Perfect timing," sneered Charlie. "You'll be collecting four gees just in time to piss it away on the same drunken broad that's been chumping ya for thirty-five years."

"Foy, you got a bigger mouth than Martha Raye, only nothing comes out of yours. Now close it up on your own p-p-power before I c-c-close it for ya."

"That'll be the day," said Foy, as he walked out of the room and damn near slammed the door off its hinges. Charlie realized now that the role he was playing was like that of a guy who breaks up a fight between a man and his wife and ends up getting clobbered by both of them. After a bit of reflection, Foy decided he had been too cruel with Joe. Sheepishly, he apologized, then said, "Joe, we don't work tonight and I have an invite to be a guest on that new gambling ship. If we're at San Pedro by seven o'clock, they'll take us to the three-mile limit, where the big ship is anchored. Dinner and wine are on the house, and for the rest of the night you're on a floating Las Vegas."

As soon as they got aboard, Joe headed for the dice table. A southpaw with his little finger in a splint threw the dice. His point was six. Joe threw a dollar on the table and shouted, "Hard s-s-six, please."

The shooter came right out with two threes. "Ah *six*—he made it the hard way," announced the croupier. "The dice are hot."

"Ride that t-t-ten, please," requested Joe—and zoom, the southpaw came right back with another pair of threes.

Frisco's single-dollar bet pyramided to one hundred bucks. He casually folded the money, turned to the stick man and said, "I'll be b-b-back. I just wanna throw a couple bucks in the ocean for luck."

When they reached the rail, Joe handed Charlie fifty bucks. "Hold this for me. I owe you at least forty bucks for my phone bill today."

Ignoring the comment about the phone bill, Foy said, "I was just looking out at that Pacific Ocean. Water, water, water. Didja ever see so much water in your life?"

"Never," agreed Frisco, "and remember: we're only seeing the t-t-top of it."

On Joe's first day at Republic, everything came up roses. The studio heads were delighted. Joe did his entire horse-betting routine. To make Joe feel right at home on the set and to help create authentic atmosphere, the studio hired a couple of local bookmakers as extras. The prop man even supplied a currently dated *Racing Form* to use in his stint. Before the day was over, Joe succeeded in using the *Racing Form* to lose sixty dollars cash and owe twenty.

A decision was made to take a four-day break before shooting the Frisco jazz dance. The dance director needed a few more days' rehearsal for the girls. Just as Ziegfeld had done many years before, they planned on backing Joe with twenty-four girls wearing leotards and bowler hats, and smoking big prop cigars. It was also decided to revive "Darktown Strutters' Ball." Joe visited a few rehearsals but kept the director off balance by constantly telling him how Loretta McDermott did the dance. He got so obnoxious building up Loretta that the director ordered him off the set and told him not to return until he received his call.

This rebuff, however, didn't stop Joe from trying to locate his old girlfriend. He enlisted the aid of everyone but the bureau of missing persons. Eventually, he located his old pal, Rasputin, consoling himself with the thought that "if Loretta is in Chicago, 'Ras' will find her."

By a stroke of good luck, Joe finished at Republic before the faithful Rasputin located Loretta. She actually was at the Grant Hotel, but not as a guest. Loretta was a hatcheck girl, working the same room in which she had been an entertainer a quarter of a century before.

"Is she well, Ras? Is she all right? Does she need help?"

"You're a little late, pal," was the response.

"What is it; is she drinking?" inquired Joe eagerly.

"Drinking?!" he repeated mockingly. "Joe, this gal has a double martini before breakfast, and then she doesn't have breakfast—she has another martini."

"Oh God!" moaned Joe. "Ya know things have been going p-p-pretty good for me lately. I'd like to help Loretta. Do you think I can p-p-pick up the pieces?"

"No, Joe, you can't pick 'em up; you'd have to sweep 'em up."

"Ras, where can I reach her?"

"Who knows?" sighed Rasputin. "After seeing her on the job last night, I don't think she'll be there tonight."

"Will you try to find her and t-t-tell her to call me c-c-collect, please?"

"Will do, Joe, but don't hold your breath until you hear from her. So long, guy."

In a state of shock, Joe reached over to put the phone on the hook, when Charlie barged in. He took one look at Frisco.

"Good gawd, what the hell happened to you?" By now the tears were streaming down Joe's cheeks. "You look like a whipped dog."

"I wish I was a d-d-dog," sobbed Joe. "I wish I was a dog and I wish you were a t-t-tree. Damn it!"

"Funny, funny, funny, Mr. Frisco, but if you can get so emotional over that broad's misfortune, ya better hang on to the bedpost, 'cause I'm gonna hit you with some real bad news."

"Oh, please," mocked Joe, dramatically wringing his hands, "don't tell me I've been d-d-drafted."

"No, funnyman, Uncle Sam doesn't want dirty old men—but he does want your money. As a matter of fact, he already took it. Republic Studio just phoned. The Collector of Internal Revenue has garnisheed your salary. Now say something funny, chum."

"All I can say is—there's hard times ahead for my b-b-bookmaker."

Two days later, Frisco and Foy were part of an inquisition in the office of the Collector of Internal Revenue. Joe was dismayed to learn that they had charts and files on him that dated back several years.

"Mr. Frisco," announced the interrogator, Mr. Flaherty, "tax evasion is one thing; fraud is another. Now let's talk. Your honest cooperation will be helpful."

"Sir," interjected Foy, "Mr. Frisco has a speech impediment, so if I may, I would like to speak for him. He's over sixty now and quite nervous."

"And I'm s-s-sick, too," cut in Joe. "I been s-s-sick for years."

"Did you say sick?" inquired Mr. Flaherty. "Strange, according to our records you attend the races practically every day."

"That's my s-s-sickness," stuttered Joe.

The stern gentleman laughed, but then said, "Okay, now let's cut the levity and get to work."

Charlie Foy took over now and was very impressive. He suggested Mr. Frisco get two thousand dollars and the government take the other two in full settlement of Joe's tax delinquency. He emphasized that Mr. Frisco was very much in debt and that with his advancing years the chance of another windfall such as he had just had at Republic Studio was remote.

After a conference in an inner office, Mr. Flaherty gave the ultimatum: Mr. Frisco would receive a thousand dollars. "The balance will go to the Tax Department, and the case will be permanently closed."

"Do you drive me to the p-p-poor house or do I take a b-b-bus?" inquired Joe sarcastically.

"May I remind you that this is the only lump sum of money you have paid the government in your entire career. You are a lucky man. Please remember that actually you owe Uncle Sam a fortune."

In the outer lobby, Joe ran into Pat Rooney Jr. Pat was worried. He owed eighty-five dollars in back taxes. Joe took Pat by the hand and said, "C-C-Come with me." He walked Junior to the office he had just left, opened the door, and shouted, "Mr. F-F-Flaherty!"

Flaherty looked up from his desk, annoyed at the undisciplined approach. Undaunted, Frisco continued. "Mr. Flaherty, this is P-P-Pat Rooney Jr. He owes you eighty-five dollars. He's broke right now, but don't worry about it—just put his b-b-bill on my t-t-tab."

While Charlie and Joe were driving home from the federal building, the tension in the car was so great, it created a steam that fogged the windshield. Finally, Joe spoke.

"Foy, no one ever accused you of tossing money around, b-b-but you did a hell of a job today with mine."

"Frisco, you don't seem to realize that you are dealing with Uncle Sam, not Aunt Minnie. You're lucky you're not rotting in jail."

"If I didn't still owe that three hundred d-d-dollars on your automobile, you'd have probably suggested that Uncle Sam keep my whole g-g-goddamn purse."

"Or—if you got the four thousand," ranted Foy, "you could have sent it to Loretta to put her through finishing school."

"You didn't go to finishing school, but you'll b-b-be finished if you make one more crack about Loretta."

"Frisco, why don't you get the hell out of this car and take a bus?"

"B-B-Because I can't afford it—thanks to you."

Joe had to go to Republic Studio to sign an authorization for them to turn over the three thousand dollars to the Collector of Internal Revenue. Joe thought he would get his one thousand dollars in cash, but the auditor could not or would not accommodate him. At this particular time Joe was reluctant about letting Charlie handle his money because he still had a stubborn urge to help Loretta. He had no place to cash a big check. Joe had no bank account. For years he'd been carrying his inventory in his pocket.

Charlie's opposition landed on deaf ears, but the collect call Joe expected came from Rasputin, not Loretta. Ras piled it on even more viciously than Charlie. "They poured Loretta back on a train to Cleveland," was the opening sentence. There was much more information, but not very comforting to Frisco. After Eddie Cox had walked out on Loretta, she had apparently had a romance with a gangster in Cleveland. It was even rumored she had married him but at the same time had eyes for the guy's partner, or vice versa.

"All I know," concluded Ras, "the two-timing created bad blood. Bad blood between two bad guys and a bad dame."

Then for a final payoff, "Joe, I beg you for the last time—forget her. Get lost. Save a little self-respect. So long, guy," and he hung up the phone. That was the conclusion of a full week of heartaches.

15

Pass the "Milltowns," Please

Joe Frisco had never been through such a heartbreaking week with no place to run. No escape. Even the horses weren't running. Both racetracks were closed, and he and Charlie Foy were at daggers drawn. The clown of the nightclubs no longer had the resilience to bounce back, as he used to. He was dull, and his performance lacked luster.

Charlie was delighted when Bing Crosby invited Joe to San Francisco, where he was shooting a picture directed by David Butler, another inveterate horseplayer. Just like Crosby, Butler was a pushover audience for Joe Frisco. He was so delighted to have Joe on the set that he wrote him into the picture. During Joe's absence, Foy had an opportunity to engage Frank Fay for four weeks at a reasonable salary, and he decided the change would be good for all concerned.

Immediately upon arrival in San Francisco, Joe snapped out of the doldrums. Butler greeted him warmly, saying, "You'll be happy with us, Joe."

"What're the odds?" asked Joe.

Well, to hear David Butler laugh at that line, one would have thought Toto the Clown had just done a backflip through a putty blower into a dish of Jello.

There were ten days of fun and laughter—till the San Francisco segment of the picture was finished. David Butler decided to give the entire cast a smashing party at a famous Italian restaurant, John's Rendezvous. The food was excellent and the red wine was potent. It was suggested that someone had spiked the wine, because everybody got feeling awfully good awfully soon. In no time, Bing was up on the dance floor with his face in the mike, singing one request after another.

Bing was just finishing one of his old favorites, "Love Thy Neighbor," when Joe Frisco walked out on the floor. He gently pushed Crosby aside, stuck his own face into the mike, and said, "This b-b-boy needs help."

David Butler was a big, hearty man, and he boomed with laughter.

Joe then turned to Crosby, pinched his cheek, and said, "You're a g-g-good boy. I'd like you to sing two choruses of 'T-T-Tea for Two' and don't show us how loud you can sing because it's more important for the folks to hear my taps." Bing momentarily became Joe's stooge and loved it; so did the diners. The applause at the finish was deafening. For an encore, Joe requested Bing to sing "The Darktown Strutters' Ball." Bing agreed to take a crack at it, and Joe replied, "If you do a good job, I'll see if I can g-g-get Big John to give you a couple of extra m-m-meatballs."

Joe did his now familiar jazz dance while Crosby did the vocalizing. At the finish, the audience went wild. They tore down the building. When Bing laughingly walked back to his table, Joe took the microphone and shouted, "Sonny boy, I guess now you know that in the future, you'll be b-b-better off if you run as part of an entry."

Big John, the restaurant owner, always sat in a large, overstuffed armchair in a location from which he could overlook the entire establishment. John enjoyed the entertainment as much as his guests did. In his Italian dialect, he said, "You good, Joe, you big hit."

Frisco said, "I'm glad you like me. How about putting me to work here for a couple weeks?"

"Is good for you to worka here," was John's rejoinder. "Is easy work; my audience is likes you very much. Food, you getta free, so how mucha you salary?"

"Well," replied Joe, with a slight yawn and very casual like. "I get a thousand a week, but since I happen to be up here in S-S-San Francisco and the racetrack is open, you can b-b-buy me for two weeks for a thousand."

"A tousand a dolla!" screamed John. "You carazy?"

Fifteen minutes later he called Joe over to his big chair. "Joe, I likea you, I likea you worka here a coupla weeks."

"What's the deal now?" asked Frisco.

"I give a you five hundred dolla for two weeks."

"You mean t-t-two fifty a week?" replied Joe disgustedly. "Hmph—I'll take it! You got a deal." Joe stuck out his hand and John hung on to it after the handshake, then added:

"Just onea more ting, Joe. You know you gotta throw dat singer in, too."

When Joe regained his composure, he explained to John who the singer was and what he made a week. John hired Joe alone. Opening night, Joe got the following telegram: "You're a fine partner. I hear you took the job without me. Crosby." After the two-week stint at the San Francisco restaurant, Joe was glad to get back to the Foy Supper Club, and Foy was equally glad to have him. Soon it would be Christmas, which to Joe meant that very soon Santa Anita would be open.

Charlie observed that Joe was beginning to slow down. After his dance routine he puffed badly. He also looked rather drawn and appeared to be losing weight. Charlie tried to get him to go for a medical checkup.

"I don't want any part of those croakers," Joe responded. "Doctors are a fake; they make you sick. The last guy I went to tapped me on the chest and said, 'Cough.' I couldn't. He tapped me again and said, 'Cough.' But I couldn't cough. Then he hit me on the back three or four times and kept saying, 'Cough, cough, cough!' Finally, I coughed a couple of times. He bent down, picked up his bag, and said, 'How long have you had that cough?'"

At the racetrack, Joe could always generate enough energy to hustle around in search of information. Opening day at Santa Anita, he ran into Jolson. Al had just picked the winner of the previous race and was feeling cocky.

"How you doin', Joe? Still picking losers?"

"I p-p-pick my share of winners, too," countered Joe.

"Have you picked the winner of the next race?" teased Al.

"Yes," boasted Joe, "I p-p-picked the winner and I ain't t-t-telling you who I p-p-picked."

"Joe, you can't pick your nose. I'll lay you fifty to twenty that after the next race you can't show me a winning ticket."

"Put the fifty where your big mouth is, 'cause you g-g-got a bet." Joe put up his twenty and Harry Akst, the songwriter, held the dough. Frisco then rushed downstairs and bought a ticket on every horse in the race. Ten two-dollar tickets. After the race, he took the winning ticket and performed his favorite stunt. He moistened the back of the ticket with his saliva, stuck it on his forehead, marched into Jolson's box, and collected his bet. He also collected twenty-two dollars at the cashier's window on the winning ticket, so he outsmarted Jolson to the tune of fifty dollars.

Even though he ended up with an unexpected fifty from Jolson, Joe was out of cash the next day. For Christmas, he had received a beautiful silk robe from Charlie. It was luxurious, to say the least, and it was still in its box. When Charlie left for the bank, Joe sneaked out with the robe under his arm. At the London Shop on Hollywood Boulevard, he went through a whole routine explaining that a silk robe was not practical for him. A flannel robe at $39.50 was just what he needed. The customer is always right! Joe got a refund of over fifty dollars, and he was ready for the second day at the races.

After several weeks of working until two A.M., then rushing to the track at noon, Joe began to look like a shadow. Charlie showed concern for Joe's health, but Joe was still reaching for laughs. "I'm all right," he insisted. "They're gonna revive *The Thin Man*, and I'm getting in shape for the part." But one day, Joe didn't feel like making the trip to Santa Anita. Instead he prevailed on Foy to take him to Connie Hurley's Horse Room, next to the Brown Derby.

At four thirty after a no-win day, Foy announced, "Joe, let's call it quits. There's six bucks left in the treasury. If we order carefully, we can have dinner at Musso Frank's."

"I have a better idea," Joe said enthusiastically. "I'm gonna make chicken c-c-cacciatore. You get the groceries and vegetables, and I'll walk over to my friend the p-p-poultry man on Santa Monica. Gimme two bucks for the chicken, and I'll meet you here in about twenty minutes."

Charlie walked to the market and got bread, butter, celery, tomatoes, and two pieces of French pastry. With the market bag under his arm, he stood and waited and waited and waited.

Two friends came by. "Dja see Frisco?" inquired Foy. "Yeah," was the reply. "He's in Connie's."

Charlie did a quick burn. As he entered he heard the calling of a race over the loudspeaker. Frisco was completely absorbed, listening intently. Charley ambled over to Joe. "Where's the chicken?"

"Sh," shushed Joe. "The chicken is leading by two lengths coming into the stretch."

One morning at breakfast, while Joe was having trouble swallowing, he confessed to Charlie that he had gone to a doctor. He admitted they had taken X-rays and found that Joe had a growth on his esophagus. The doctor said it was the size of a golf ball.

"Well, are you going to let him operate?" Charlie inquired.

"Hell, no," said Joe, still trying for laughs. "It's only a golf ball. I was standing in the fairway and saw Jack Benny hit a ball off the tee. He really connected, a b-b-beautiful shot. I opened my mouth in amazement and kerplunk, the g-g-golf b-b-ball landed in my throat. Now Jack Benny is just hoping I'll have the operation so that he can get back his golf ball."

16

"Hya, Doc, Who Do Ya Like?"

Joe made only one more trip to Santa Anita. On that day he met Marcus Rabwin, a famous surgeon. Marc owned a couple of thoroughbreds and was a friend of Charlie Foy. Joe greeted him with his usual salutation, "Hya, Doc, who do ya like?" The good doctor took one look at Joe Frisco, put his arm around him, and said, "Joe, I want to see you in my office at ten o'clock tomorrow morning."

By noon the next day, Joe was in Cedars of Lebanon Hospital. Two days later, he was in surgery. Through Dr. Rabwin's assistance, Joe was operated on by a renowned specialist. He got wonderful care, but obviously Joe had waited too long. He didn't respond, and several weeks later, he was moved to the Motion Picture Country Home.

The first day, when he was helped to his room, his nurse said, "Mr. Frisco, take off your clothes, get in the bed, and I'll be right with you."

"That's what they all say," cracked Joe, "b-b-but I always end up alone."

When the staff doctor asked Joe if he was comfortable and being well taken care of, Joe said he wished he could get a male nurse. "That d-d-dame is no help. She can't even read a *Racing Form*."

Joe was an awful coward, so when it was time for the doctor to swab Joe's infected throat, Joe tried vainly to talk the doctor out of it. After the ordeal, the doctor said kindly:

"Now that didn't hurt too much, did it?"

Said Joe, "Ya heard me holler, didn't ya? Well, I wasn't selling papers."

It was said of Joe that when many of his imitators were making money, all he made was friends. Nowhere have more friends congregated daily than in Joe Frisco's hospital room. Most of them were comics who came to entertain Joe, but sick as he was, Joe himself couldn't stop reaching for laughs.

"HYA, DOC, WHO DO YA LIKE?"

No illness could keep him from trying to retain his rating as top banana.

After the weekly *Variety* carried the story of Joe's illness and his move to the Motion Picture Home, he was inundated with mail and phone calls from all over the country. On one occasion, while several of his pals were visiting, comedian Myron Cohen called from New York. Joe Kirk answered the phone. Cupping his hand over the mouthpiece, he said, "It's Myron Cohen calling, Joe. He's asking what's wrong with you."

"T-T-Tell him I had a shot glass removed from my throat," was Joe's suggestion.

Kirk continued talking and finished the conversation by saying, "No, Myron, thanks very much, uh huh, that's very nice of you but no, Myron, he doesn't."

Kirk hung up the phone and then explained to Joe, "That Myron Cohen guy is quite persistent. He wanted to know for sure that you didn't need any money. I told him no, you didn't."

"You told him no? Well, thank you very m-m-much, Mr. Big Shot." Joe then lifted up his pillow and said, "Look pal, d-d-do you see any ham sandwiches hiding under there?"

There were always so many visitors in his room accompanied by such an abundance of laughter that one of the gang thought up a brilliant idea: why not give a Joe Frisco testimonial dinner at one of the big clubs? Joe was thrilled over the idea. The guys at the Masquers Club were the most enthusiastic and had open dates. All that was necessary now was to get the approval of the staff at the Motion Picture Country Home. Joe still harbored an old fear. "Make sure you get their p-p-permission before we go. I don't want to come all the way b-b-back and find I've been locked out of my room."

The staff said if arrangements could be made to take Mr. Frisco from the home to the Masquers Club by private ambulance, they would approve. They would also send along a competent nurse who could be in attendance en route and during the dinner.

The Masquers announced the affair as "Joe Frisco Night" in honor of the beloved comic. Within three days every available space was reserved. "I want this to be a fun night," Joe insisted.

It was a fun night. Harry Joe Brown, Chief Harlequin of the Masquers Club, started the evening's festivities with the usual formalities. He paid tribute to Joe Frisco and then introduced comedian Pat Buttram, who was the master of ceremonies for the entire affair. Pat read dozens of humorous telegrams, including one from Jack Benny, which he claimed came collect. The ribbing started immediately, and it evolved into a hilarious roast. Joe Frisco sat on the side of the stage in a wheelchair. Attached to the chair was a microphone that enabled Joe to cut in on the ribbing and roasting whenever he felt the urge.

Buttram apologized for the absence of cowboy star Gene Autry, with whom he had been associated for many years. "I played his pal," commented Pat. "Always, as Gene rode off into the sunset, I rode behind him. For seven years all I looked at was the rear end of Gene Autry's horse. Tonight as I look out at this huge audience—hm—all that's missing is the sunset."

Pat's first introduction brought on Joe's sidekick, comic Cully Richards. As soon as Pat said the name, Frisco groaned.

"Oh God, I thought this was going to be a *fun* show."

"Don't mind him, folks," said Cully. "He's delirious. I've spent a lot of time with Joe at the hospital and he's become a noodlehead. He applauds the nurse when she takes out the bedpan."

Cully recounted the daily carryings-on in Joe's hospital room, referring to it as a laugh factory. Some of the details, including an account of Joe's incontinence, got quite gamy.

"Ah," shouted Frisco, "my good friend, Cully, he has such g-g-good taste—ich!"

Cully continued: "One day, we were sitting and trading lies about horses and broads. The nurse came in and told Joe it was time to give him a transfusion. She set up the apparatus and then told me to get lost for several hours so Joe would be quiet. After I left, the nurse also left the room and in walked three more guys. They were having laughs while I sat outside biting my fingernails. When I returned, I noticed that the glass container with the transfusion was still three-quarters full; so I pressed the button for the nurse. She was surprised to see all the company and said, 'What are you having here, Mr. Frisco, a convention?'"

"No," Joe countered, "the boys are rehearsing for my wake. How much longer is it going to take to get the rest of this stuff in my veins? You said t-t-two hours. Most of the juice is still up there in the bottle."

"My guess," said the nurse, "is *one* hour."

"My guess," mocked Cully, "is *two* hours."

"Why don't we bet?" suggested Joe. "I'll make book."

"I've a better idea," cut in Jim Wright. "Let's make a pool."

"Good deal," approved Joe Kirk. "Let's throw in a buck apiece. My bet is on one hour and thirty minutes," and he threw a dollar bill on the bed.

"I still stand on my original guess of two hours," said Cully, throwing in his dollar.

Frisco turned to Foy. "P-P-Put me up for a buck, will ya? I b-b-bet on sixty-five minutes."

The nurse walked toward the bed and Frisco said, "Uh uh, now she wants to get in on it."

The good-natured nurse said, "I'll put in fifty cents."

"Oh no," Joe protested. "It's a buck or nuthin'." Then he whispered to Jim Wright, "I don't trust this dame."

Wright then threw in his buck and declared, "My bet is on seventy minutes."

Ignoring all their nonsensical predictions, the nurse walked over to Joe's bed, adjusted the apparatus, and immediately the liquid started to gurgle and flow out of the bottle.

"What did I tell you?" shouted Joe. "This dame knows something."

Now they all watched eagerly, and in twenty minutes the bottle was empty. Joe grabbed the money and shouted, "INQUIRY! I d-d-demand an inquiry!"

At this moment a tall German nurse walked in carrying a container. "Okay boys," she commanded, "Out—everybody—OUT!"

"Yeah," agreed Joe. "I'm about to get an *enema*, and there will be no b-b-bets on that."

After Cully made his exit, Pat Buttram introduced Charlie Foy, but all he got from him was a bow. Being highly emotional, Charlie didn't trust himself to talk for fear he would blubber. Frisco decided to talk for him.

"I worked for this Foy guy for fifteen years. When one o'clock Monday arrived, we'd all sit at a round table in the basement and he'd p-p-pay off. One day he laid my salary on the table and a little ant with a double hernia carried it away."

Next came Jack Dempsey, who tried to figure out how long he'd known

Joe Frisco. "We first met in 1930. Let me see, now, 1930 until 1940 is ten years, and then until—"

That was as far as Dempsey got. Joe groaned, "There goes that long count again."

Jack laughed, "I can't top this guy. I want you to know that when folks call me a champ in the presence of a man like our honored guest, I blush. Joe is a real champ."

Next, Jack Pepper sang his heart out for his old pal. When Pepper finished "If I Had My Life to Live Over," Joe wiped away a tear.

Pat now brought on Morey Amsterdam. He got a great many laughs. Then turning to Joe, Morey said, "I'm not much of a horseplayer but when I do gamble, I'm really a plunger."

"You're a p-p-plunger, eh? I'll remember that," shouted Joe. "The next time the t-t-toilet gets stopped, we'll c-c-call you."

While a nurse gave Frisco some medicine, Pat Buttram introduced many more celebrities and told some hilarious stories.

Former headliner Julius Tannen, then seventy-seven, was extraordinary. This old master of comedy explained how cleverly Joe Frisco employed his stutter as an instrument to punch over his humor.

Again Joe got into the act. "Hey, Julius," he shouted, "how about the big tall guy in the movies, G-G-Gary Cooper? All I've ever heard him say was 'Yup,' 'Nope,' and 'Uh huh' and he gets t-t-ten thousand dollars a week. Can you imagine what his salary would be if he could say a sentence like—er—'D-D-Does your husband know how we f-f-feel about each other?'"

Old friend Cliff Edwards thanked Joe for giving him his first real job.

Walter Winchell said he could echo Cliff's words. "Joe was making five thousand dollars a week while I was an aspiring columnist. I had one of his quotes under my byline almost every day. I'm proud again to thank him publicly." Then Winchell continued, "The first Frisco story I used is a sort of commentary on this changing world. It was in the days when every other entertainer was imitating Al Jolson. There was a group of Jolson imitators loafing in front of the Palace Theatre. It included George Jessel, Mel Klee, Buddy Walker, Buddy Doyle, Georgie Price, and a few other guys who used to put on burnt cork and white gloves and get down on one knee and sing

'Mammy.' As Joe passed, he looked at the group, flicked his cigar, and said, 'Hya, Al,' and kept right on walking."

After tossing Joe a few more gracious compliments, Winchell bowed off. The nurse then whispered in Pat Buttram's ear. Pat turned to the audience and said, "Gentlemen, we're running a little long." Now Joe spoke up.

"M-m-much too long. My act never ran over t-t-twenty minutes, until they got me on the operating table. What a ham that d-d-doctor was. He kept c-c-cutting up for three hours."

Wally Ford interrupted. Holding a drink in his hand, he walked to the microphone and said, "May I say a toast to my dear friend, Joe?"

This was the first time in many years that anyone saw the famous character actor without his beard. He raised his glass and said, "Joe, I drink to your health when I'm with you. I drink to your health when alone. I drank to your health so doggone much, I damn near ruined my own."

"Thank you," said Joe, "but who the hell are you?"

Buttram spoke up, "Joe, I was just as confused as you. For once I couldn't tell a Ford from an Edsel. This is your old friend Wally Ford, without his beard."

"Good heavens," exclaimed Joe, "b-b-bless ya, Wally, and shame on me, but I'm glad there are no b-b-beards at the table tonight or I'd swear to God it was the Last Supper."

The guests howled. Little did they know that once again, Joe had had the last laugh. It was Joe's last supper.

Several days later, most of these same men and many more were paying tribute to Joe Frisco. On this occasion in 1958 there was no laughter. Joe Frisco was silent.

Only one voice was audible. As if coming from heaven, the voice of Jack Pepper could be heard by the mourners as he sang "There Must Be a Heaven for Clowns."

PEOPLE AND PLACES: A GLOSSARY

"LORETTA, HOW COULD YOU?"
AN ESSAY ON CHRONOLOGY

SELECTED BIBLIOGRAPHY

INDEX

People and Places
A Glossary

Akst, Harry (1893–1963): songwriter; appeared in a few films; started career with Irving Berlin; wrote a number of popular songs—for example, "Baby Face"—and production tunes; toured USO camps with Al Jolson, who died in his arms in San Francisco.

Albee, Edward Franklin (1857–1930): theatre impresario; ran the B. F. Keith chain of theatres and, during his heyday, monopolized booking arrangements; one of the giants in vaudeville management; uniformly disliked for being authoritarian, parsimonious, and inflexible.

Allen, Fred (1894–1956): started his career as a writer for *Variety*, then turned comedian; played vaudeville, went on to Broadway, and then appeared on radio, where his show "Allen's Alley"—in which he interviewed a series of ethnic characters—had an enormous following.

Amsterdam, Morey (1914–1996): actor, writer, composer; appeared on radio, in nightclubs, and on television; wrote a number of songs, including "Rum and Coca Cola."

Andrews, Lois (Lorraine Gourley) (1924–1968): chorus line dancer; at her "sweet 16" birthday party in New York, March 24, 1940, she proudly exhibited Jessel's engagement ring; married three weeks later in Detroit, they were divorced thirty-three months later.

Arbuckle, Roscoe "Fatty" (1887–1933): comic silent movie star; in 1913 joined Mack Sennett's Keystone Cops; subsequently wrote and directed many of his own films; in 1921, acting career ruined by a sex scandal.

Arcaro, Eddie (1916–1997): jockey, television commentator; only jockey to have ridden two Triple Crown winners; during career rode more than four thousand winners; member of Racing Hall of Fame; subsequently a television commentator of major races.

Arlington Park (racetrack): Chicago, Illinois; pioneered racing on grass; major races are the American Derby, the Secretariat Stakes, the Arlington Classic, and the Arlington Washington Futurity.

Astaire, Fred (1899–1987): dancer, choreographer, singer, actor, who moved from vaudeville to Broadway to films; left his mark on the song-and-dance film; audiences adored his dancing and acting partnership with Ginger Rogers, which lasted ten years.

Astor Hotel: New York; located at 1515 Broadway, between Forty-fourth and Forty-fifth; a luxurious hotel, with a large cabaret on the roof called the Roof Garden.

Atlantic City (1944): musical film (Republic Pictures); cast included Louie Armstrong, Paul Whiteman, and Joe Frisco; unoriginal plot about a promoter who turns the Atlantic City pier into "the playground of America."

Autry, Gene (1907–): started as a singer, entered films as a singing cowboy, and eventually had his own radio show, film production company, and baseball team, the Los Angeles Angels.

Baby Snooks: See **Brice, Fanny**.

Baer, Arthur "Bugs" (1886–1969): columnist, cartoonist, humorist; wrote the column "One Word Led to Another"; credited with being responsible for many gags and stories used in the routines of top comedians.

Barrymore, John (1882–1942): actor; started as a painter and cartoonist; played stage comedy roles as well as Shakespeare; famous for his modernized portrayal of Hamlet (1923); appeared in silent and sound films but didn't like the medium; called the "Great Profile."

Bayes, Nora (Eleanor Goldberg) (1880–1928): Once billed as "the greatest single woman singing comedienne in the world"; had an extensive repertoire of songs that ranged from semi-classics to comedy; appeared in a number of Broadway shows, made numerous recordings, and gave generously of her time to benefits and to wartime entertainment for the troops.

Bay View (born 1937): racehorse; as a 58–1 longshot, won the Santa Anita Handicap in 1941, receiving the longest price ever paid for the winner of this race: $118.40 for a two-dollar bet.

BeeHee and Rubyatte: troupe of six Arab acrobats; their act included sock tumbling and pyramid building, accompanied by Middle Eastern music and tom-toms.

Belmont Park (racetrack): Elmont, Long Island, New York; opened in 1890; known for Belmont Stakes, third race in the Triple Crown (preceded by the Kentucky Derby and Preakness); attracts the best horses in the East.

Benny, Jack (1894–1974): celebrated comedian of radio, television, and occasional films; famous for his pretended stinginess, his screechy violin playing, and his never-changing age of thirty-nine; one of the first to use the comedy of self-deprecation.

Bent, Marion (1879–1940): performed with her husband, Pat Rooney Jr., in a pop-

GLOSSARY

ular song-and-dance routine; known for their hospitality, the couple maintained a New York apartment that was a nightly gathering place for managers, agents, and vaudevillians; she retired early because of arthritis.

Berle, Milton (1908–): comedian; began in vaudeville, appeared on Broadway, and became an immensely popular television performer ("Uncle Milty"); made a few films, which enjoyed only a modest success.

Berlin, Irving (1888–1989): one of America's most popular songwriters; built the Music Box Theatre; wrote music for Broadway hits *Annie Get Your Gun* (1946) and *Call Me Madam* (1950); composed music for films, notably *Top Hat* (1935), *Follow the Fleet* (1936), and *Carefree* (1938); his single biggest song hit was "White Christmas" (1942).

Bijou Dream Theatre: Ashland, Wisconsin; located at 310 West Second, now called Main Street.

Biscailuz, Eugene W. (1883–1969): Sheriff, Los Angeles County, 1932–1958; a little man with a courtly manner who was "Mr. California" to his law officers; a crack shot and skilled rider, he liked to wear a wide-brimmed hat and appear in parades at the side of Hollywood celebrities.

Brice, Fanny (1891–1951): regarded as one of the greatest singing comediennes in American theatre; a natural pantomimist who could, with a look or gesture, reduce her audience to hysterics; played the mischievous brat Baby Snooks on the stage and then on the radio.

Brooks, Shelton Leroy (1886–1975): African American composer and lyricist; spent about fifty years as a vaudevillian in the United States and Canada and toured Europe with Lew Leslie's *Blackbirds;* also appeared in Ken Murray's *Blackouts;* wrote "The Darktown Strutters' Ball," "Walkin' the Dog," "Honey Gal," and other songs.

Brown, Harry Joe (1890–1972): actor and director; worked in traveling companies, stock, vaudeville, and Broadway revues; in 1920 turned to directing and producing films.

Brown Derby: Hollywood; originally called the Brown Derby Cafe and located at 1628 North Vine Street, at the corner of Hollywood Boulevard.

Buchanon, Irving Agency: Chicago; booked performances into the Verdi Theatre on Thirty-fifth Street for the very good reason that Mr. Buchanon managed and owned the theatre.

Buck, Edward Eugene (1885–1957): began by designing covers for sheet music and then went on to write lyrics for many of the Ziegfeld *Follies;* became famous as the person in charge of tryouts and rehearsals for Ziegfeld.

Busher (born 1942): racehorse; in 1944 named national champion two-year-old filly; in 1945 bought by Louis B. Mayer; named horse of the year in 1945.

Bushman, Francis X. (1883–1966): actor; started in stock and moved to silent films, where he became a matinee idol (once called the handsomest man in the world); later appeared in radio soap operas and small cinematic sound roles.

Butler, David (1894–1979): silent screen actor, director; began acting in 1913 and directing in 1927; remembered for his direction of four Shirley Temple films; an avid sports fan; an honorary member of the Directors Guild.

Butterfield Circuit: one of the many smaller vaudeville circuits; excluding Chicago, found throughout the Midwest, and especially in Michigan; frequently booked "tabs"—tabloid musical comedies (i.e., shorter versions) that stayed in town a full week or two, changing their shows two and three times a week.

Buttram, Pat (1915–1994): comic actor; appeared for years as Gene Autry's screen sidekick; played the role of a sophisticated rube; employed wise and witty Will Rogers–type comedy; had a long television run as Mr. Haney in *Green Acres*.

Caliente (racetrack): Tijuana, Mexico (twenty miles south of San Diego); originally called Agua Caliente; opened in 1929; famous for its "5–10 Pool," where bettors make selections for six consecutive races on a single ticket.

Cantor, Eddie (1892–1964): pop-eyed singer-comedian; began in vaudeville and became famous on Broadway as a blackface comedian; during Depression moved to radio, with a listening audience of sixty million; in Hollywood, made films and appeared on television; a major force in show business for fifty years.

Carroll, Earl (1893–1948): lyricist turned producer; found fame with his *Vanities* of 1923, and later editions; built two theatres, both of which he named for himself.

Carus, Emma (1879–1927): singer with a big, deep voice; could move from a contralto to a baritone and sing in numerous dialects; alternated between the legitimate stage and vaudeville.

Caruso, Enrico (1873–1921): Italian operatic tenor; during his day considered the greatest tenor in the world; appeared in a few silent films.

Casimir Theatre: Chicago; located at 4750 Milwaukee Avenue; opened 1922; seated 491.

Catlett, Walter (1889–1960): actor and comedian; noted for his comic prop, a pair of tortoiseshell glasses (owing to poor eyesight); started acting at thirteen; worked for Ziegfeld; in 1929 entered films; an inveterate gambler.

Cedars of Lebanon Hospital: Los Angeles; located originally at 4833 Fountain Avenue; now called Cedars Sinai and bounded by Beverly, Third, San Vincente, and Robertson.

Chaplin, Sir Charles Spencer "Charlie" (1889–1977): pantomimist, actor, director,

GLOSSARY

producer, screenwriter, composer; his silent films now considered classics, but only a few of his later sound films are; became the greatest screen clown of all time with his impersonation of a tramp.

Chaplin, Sydney John Hill (1885–1965): Charlie's older half brother and, beginning in 1916, partner; managed Charlie briefly; comic actor; appeared in films and performed on cruise ships.

Charlie Foy Supper Club: Sherman Oaks, California, in the San Fernando Valley; located at 15463 Ventura Boulevard; a cavernous place about two hundred yards west of Sepulveda, on the north side of the street; currently a parking lot.

Charney, C. King (1893?–1958): film pioneer; for many years associated with Carl Laemmle in the old Universal Company; later worked with Trem Carr as an independent producer; Hollywood representative for AGFA Raw Film Corporation; hotel owner.

Chasen, Dave (1899–1973): Hollywood restaurateur, with premises at corner of Beverly Boulevard (no. 9039) and Doheny; former comic vaudevillian and Broadway performer; friend of celebrities; became the preeminent caterer to Hollywood's movie colony.

Chevalier, Albert (1862–1923): British actor, singer, author, composer; became known as the "Coster Laureate," owing to the popularity of his cockney songs; wrote most of his own words and some of the music.

Chevalier, Albert (son) (1899–1959): vaudeville comedian and comic actor; in the manner of his father, affected a cockney accent and portrayed English working-class characters.

Chi-Chi Club: Palm Springs, California; located at 217 North Palm Canyon Drive.

Choen, Carl (?–1986): casino manager at the original El Rancho Vegas; part owner of the Sands Hotel, where he gained fame by knocking down Frank Sinatra during an altercation; worked for the Hughes Corporation; ended his career as a host at MGM.

Clarke, Grant (1891–1931): lyricist, songwriter, publisher; wrote lyrics for Ziegfeld *Follies;* composed stage scores, film and popular songs; created special material for Fannie Brice, Eva Tanguay, Al Jolson, and others.

Club 18: New York; nightclub on Fifty-second Street; clientele included a great many show business people drawn to the first-rate ad-libbing "insult" comedians who performed there in groups; the comedians each had a microphone in which they cross-fired jibes and gags; Jack White (1893–1942) was the famous emcee.

Cocoanut Grove: Los Angeles; the nightclub housed in the Ambassador Hotel, located at 3400 Wilshire Boulevard.

Cohen, Myron (1902?–1986): comedian; started in the Yiddish theatre; told dialect stories with a great deadpan delivery; appeared in nightclubs and on television; wrote the book *Laughing Out Loud*.

Cook, Joe Lopez (1890–1959): began as a juggler on ice skates and a comedian; used zany inventions onstage; mastered wire walking, knife throwing, ball walking, dancing, and playing sundry musical instruments; had a wonderful way with monologue; appeared in Earl Carroll's *Vanities, Rain or Shine, Fine and Dandy*.

Cooper, Gary (1901–1961): started out as a cowboy and cartoonist; began acting in two-reelers and progressed to stardom as the quintessential slow-speaking, deep-thinking American man of action and few words; had an off-screen reputation as a great Hollywood lover.

Costello, Lou (1906–1959): first appeared in vaudeville and burlesque; in 1931 teamed up with Bud Abbott to form one of the most successful comedy teams in show business; Abbott played the straight man and Costello the funnyman.

Cox, Eddie (1894–1958): song-and-dance performer; started as a child actor with the Dockstader and Primrose Minstrels; later teamed with Joe Frisco; after vaudeville played nightclubs.

Creole Cafe: New Orleans; no information available.

Crosby, Bing (1901–1977): pop singer, actor; career encompassed virtually every facet of entertainment world but legitimate theatre—presentation houses, nightclubs, radio, recordings, film, and television; Oscar winner (1944); called "The Groaner" and "Der Bingle."

Curtis, Jack (1881?–1949): legendary vaudeville and Hollywood agent; managed such greats as Durante, Jessel, Sophie Tucker, and Gypsy Rose Lee; began as a "Dutch" comic; produced *The Postman Rings Twice* and a few other plays.

Cypress Hills Cemetery: Brooklyn, New York; located at 833 Jamaica Avenue.

Cyrano de Bergerac: brave, romantic, poetic hero of a play of the same name (1897) by Edmond Rostand; deformed by a grotesquely large nose, he woos the beautiful Roxanne for another man while loving her himself.

Daily Racing Form: founded 1894; a daily morning paper, currently published in Highstown, New Jersey; often referred to as "racing's bible"; lists race entries, results, and past performances of horses running that day; also distances, times, track conditions, jockeys, and prospects of winning.

Dale, Charles (Joseph Sultzer) (1881–1971): comedian; started Avon Comedy Four with Joe Smith; appeared with Smith in "Dr. Kronkhite" skit, which always made the "ten best" list of vaudeville dream bills; cared about welfare of other actors, working on their behalf as board member of the American Guild of Variety Actors.

GLOSSARY

Damon and Pythias (classical legend): friends so devoted to each other that when Pythias, who had been condemned to death, asked leave to arrange his affairs, Damon pledged his life that his friend would return.

Darling, Edward V. (1890–1951): began as confidential secretary to E. F. Albee and rose to become chief booker for all Keith theatres, including the Palace; unlike Albee and Keith, he had a reputation for fairness and kindness.

Davies, Marion (1897–1961): made her stage debut at sixteen in a Broadway chorus line; featured in the Ziegfeld *Follies* of 1916; began acting in silent films; became famous as the protégée and mistress of William Randolph Hearst.

Davis, Bette (1908–1989): film actress; her unique style, with its clipped speech and flamboyant manner, won her two Academy Awards, for *Dangerous* (1935) and *Jezebel* (1938); known for her portrayal of unlikable characters; in 1977 won the American Film Institute's Life Achievement Award, the first woman so honored.

Davis Theatre: Pittsburgh; located at 532 and 534 Smithfield Street; the house manager, Eugene Connolly, was notorious; Sophie Tucker declared, "It's not going too far to say that the Davis Theatre was hated by every performer in the business. Lots of them refused to play it" (DiMeglio, 1973).

DeLacey, Kitty: no information available.

Del Mar Park (racetrack): Del Mar, California; "where the turf meets the surf"; opened 1937; introduced first use of the photo-finish camera (1937); started by Bing Crosby and some associates; a favorite of the movie colony.

Del Rio, Dolores (1905–1983): beautiful Mexican film actress; appeared in silent and sound films; in 1943 returned to Mexico, where her stage and screen career blossomed.

Dempsey, Jack (1895–1983): boxer; world heavyweight champion from 1919 to 1926; nicknamed the "Manassa Mauler"; in 1927 lost to Gene Tunney after flooring him and then failing to return to his corner (the famous "long count").

Desert Hot Springs: southern California spa; located approximately ten miles north of Palm Springs.

Dixieland Five: in New Orleans called "Brown's Band from Dixieland" and led by Tom "Red" Brown; the band, paradoxically composed of six players—Ray Lopez (cornet), Tom Brown (trombone), Gus Mueller (clarinet), Arnold Loyacano (guitar), Steve Brown (bass viol), and Bill Lambert (drums)—changed names in Chicago (1915).

Dove, Billie (Lillian Bohny) (1900–1997): model, actress; among the loveliest leading ladies of Hollywood's silent era; publicized as the "American Beauty";

appeared in sound films but was unable to adapt to the new medium; retired 1932.

Doyle, Buddy (1901–1939): singer and comedian; appeared in musicals and films; famous for his impersonations of Eddie Cantor, whom he played in the film *The Great Ziegfeld* (1936).

"Dr. Kronkhite": a skit about doctors and medicine *(Krankheit* in German means *sickness)*, performed by Joe Smith and Charles Dale.

Dubuque Opera House: Dubuque, Iowa; official name the Grand Opera House; still running; located at Eighth and Iowa Streets.

Duggan, Tom (1915–1969): muckraking sports reporter, columnist, interviewer on television; had his own television show, conducting abrasive, controversial interviews (one of the first to use this technique); acted in stock theatre.

Durante, James Francis "Jimmy" (1893–1980): comedian and pianist; famous for his big nose; Cantor once said, "Jimmy has a heart as big as his schnozzola"; performed in vaudeville, Broadway musicals, nightclubs, radio, and television.

Earl Carroll Theatre: New York; located at the southeast corner of Seventh Avenue and Fiftieth Street; opened on July 5, 1923, for Earl Carroll's *Vanities* of 1923; eventually converted into a theatre and restaurant and then just a restaurant.

Edwards, Cliff (1895–1971): singer, actor; known as Ukulele Ike; a vaudeville headliner; moved on to Broadway in George White's *Scandals;* appeared in films; introduced song "Singin' in the Rain" (1927); screen voice of Jiminy Cricket.

Edwards, Gus (1879–1945): songwriter and producer; wrote "In My Merry Oldsmobile" and "By the Light of the Silvery Moon"; organized vaudeville acts consisting entirely of youngsters, many of whom went on to become famous.

Edwards, Hank: no information available.

Edwards, Rubber Legs (?): an eccentric dancer who would repeatedly fall down, get up, and fall down again, presumably because his legs couldn't support him.

Errol, Leon (1881–1951): comedian; famous for his rubber-legged drunk scenes; appeared in the Ziegfeld *Follies* and other Broadway shows; wrote and directed a number of shows and, in later years, acted in film shorts.

Fairbanks, Douglas (1883–1939): flamboyant actor known for his leaps and jumps; played in a number of Broadway shows before turning to films, where he appeared as a romantic, dashing hero.

Fay, Frank (1897–1961): started acting as a child; became an onstage storyteller of daffy yarns; found fame on Broadway in *Harvey* (1950) as the drunk Elwood P. Dowd, whose best friend is an invisible rabbit.

Feinberg, Nate (?): a small-time Chicago theatre agent; until 1938 office located at 420 Surf; then moved to 522 West Wellington.

GLOSSARY

Fields, W. C. (1879–1946): actor, screenwriter; began his stage career as a juggler, moving on to comedian and stuntman; appeared in silent and sound films; later became a cult figure for his acerbic comedy roles.

Fitzgerald, Harry (1881?–1936): leading talent agent for more than twenty years; launched new styles in acts and entertainment; said to have introduced jazz to New York; discovered Paul Whiteman, booked Will Rogers for Ziegfeld, and represented, among others, W. C. Fields and Bill Robinson.

Fitzgerald, Leo (1890?–1968): theatrical agent; brought into the business by his older brother Harry; represented headliners from vaudeville but mostly the legitimate stage; clients included Bert Wheeler and Robert Woolsey.

Ford, Wally (1898–1966): character actor; started in vaudeville; appeared on Broadway, often as the lead, before going on to Hollywood in 1930, where he played in more than two hundred films.

Foy, Bryan "Brynie" (1896–1977): producer, director; popular on the vaudeville circuit as one of the "Seven Little Foys"; in 1918 became a director of comedy shorts and free-lanced as a screenwriter and gag writer; later moved into directing and, finally, producing; directed *Lights of New York* (1928), promoted by the studio as "the first one hundred percent all-talking picture."

Foy, Eddie, Jr. (1905–1983): actor, dancer; started in vaudeville; in 1929 made his Broadway debut in Ziegfeld's *Show Girl;* appeared in numerous films in supporting roles.

Foy, Eddie, Sr. (1854–1928): stage comic and musical comedy actor; acquired fame by his exceptional mimicry, drollery, pantomimic clowning, and eccentric dancing; in 1910 brought his seven children into his vaudeville act, which became known as "Eddie Foy and the Seven Little Foys."

Foy, Mary (1905?–1987): one of "Seven Little Foys" act; third youngest of Eddie Foy's seven children; appeared with her husband, Lyle Latell, in burlesque and regional theatres; helped her brother run the Charlie Foy Supper Club.

Friars Club: New York; located at 57 East Fifty-fifth; the leading fraternal association of entertainers; a favorite meeting place of performers; hosts dinners, celebrity luncheons, and bawdy roasts to raise money for charity.

Fritzel, Michael J. (1881?–1956): Chicago restaurateur and nightclub owner; colorful career spanned over half a century; said to have invented the nightclub when he opened the Arsonia (Madison Street), frequented by Lillian Russell, Gentleman Jim Corbett, and Francis X. Bushman.

Frolics Cafe: Chicago; located at 18 East Twenty-second Street; Mike Fritzel's all-night notorious Prohibition spot, with dancing until dawn, where all the notables hung out.

Generaux, Fenn: no information available.

Georgia Street Receiving Hospital: Los Angeles; located at 1337 Georgia Street, between Pico and Venice Boulevards; the receiving hospital of Los Angeles.

Glaser, Joseph "Joe" G. (1897–1969): theatrical agent, fight promoter, dog breeder, Yankee fan; moved from Chicago to New York, eventually becoming president of Associated Booking Corporation (ABC), which managed, among others, Louis "Satchmo" Armstrong and, in the variety field, Barbra Streisand.

Gleason, Jackie (1916–1987): actor, composer, arranger, conductor; performed in vaudeville, carnivals, nightclubs, roadhouses, and films; after several Broadway outings found his niche in television, particularly in *The Honeymooners.*

Gone with the Wind (1939): film based on 1936 novel by Margaret Mitchell; starred Clark Gable and Vivian Leigh; often called the most popular motion picture ever made.

Gorilla, The (1931): contrary to Ed Lowry's statement, this film was in fact released; produced by First National, directed by Bryan Foy, and starring, among others, Joe Frisco (See "Review of *The Gorilla*," *New York Times*, February 23, 1931, 20).

Grant, Cary (1904–1986): born in England; joined a troupe of acrobats at thirteen; worked as a song-and-dance man and juggler; appeared on Broadway; in 1932 went into films, becoming an appealing straight romantic leading man and a polished performer in sophisticated comedies.

Grant Hotel: Chicago; located at 6 North Dearborn; known for its generosity and kindness to actors; the basement bar, serving beer and shrimp, was a favorite.

Grauman, Sid (1879–1950): show business impresario who built the Chinese Theatre on Hollywood Boulevard and immortalized stars via their hand- and footprints in the cement in front of the theatre; originated the gala Hollywood premiere, with its klieg lights, stars, and sidewalk crowds of fans.

Great Northern Hotel: Chicago; located at northeast corner of South Dearborn Street (no. 237) and Jackson Boulevard; a rendezvous for war veterans and veterans' organizations; widely known for its "Silver Dollar Bar," decorated with silver dollars, for its oyster house in the white marble basement, and for catering to playgoers during intermission at the Great Northern Theatre.

Great Northern Theatre: Chicago; located at 21 West Quincy; opened November 9, 1896, as a legitimate theatre; reopened August 27, 1898, as a vaudeville house; name changed to Lyric, February 1910; name changed to Hippodrome, November 11, 1912; returned to original name September 1921; closed 1961.

Green Mill Gardens: Chicago; located at 4806 North Broadway; afterward the site of the Palladium Dance Hall; fronted by Tom Chamales, a well-known 1930s

GLOSSARY

nightlife impresario, but actually owned by gangsters, who mutilated Joe E. Lewis for signing to perform elsewhere.

Hanlon, Bert (1895–1972): composer, author, actor, director; appeared in vaudeville, Broadway musicals, and films; wrote "Mississippi," "Far Far Away in Rockaway," and "I'd Love to Be a Monkey in the Zoo."

Harding, Warren Gamaliel (1865–1923): twenty-ninth president of the United States from 1921 to 1923; died in office; his administration was characterized by cronyism and corruption.

Harrington, Pat (1901?–1965): comedian; helped catapult the insult type of comedy into an important industry; instrumental in making Club 18 on New York's Fifty-second Street one of the most popular comedy rooms.

Hearst, William Randolph (1863–1951): Newspaper magnate said to be the inspiration for *Citizen Kane* (1941); founded Cosmopolitan Pictures for the sole purpose of promoting his protégée, Marion Davies.

Hialeah Racecourse: Hialeah, Florida; in Frisco's day, best-known race was the Flamingo Stakes for three-year-olds.

Hildegarde (Hildegarde Loretta Sell) (1906–): singer, pianist, comedienne; developed a popular supper club act; had her own radio show in the 1940s, the time of her greatest popularity.

Hodkins Booking Agency: Oklahoma City, Oklahoma; the booking office of the Hodkins Lyric Vaudeville Circuit, which normally booked performers for twelve- to fourteen-week engagements throughout the Southwest.

Hollywood Comedy Club: Founded in March 1947 as a fraternal organization "by a group of great and near great from the wonderful era of vaudeville"; current address, 649 North Rossmore Avenue, Los Angeles.

Hollywood Park (racetrack): Inglewood, California; opened 1938; one of the leading U.S. tracks in attendance and purses; here Citation won the Hollywood Gold Cup to become the first horse ever to win more than one million dollars.

Holtz, Lou (1898–1980): comedian, singer, producer; a consummate storyteller and dialectician; set a record for the longest continuous single attraction at the Palace, 13 weeks, in 1931; appeared on Broadway, in films, on radio, and on television.

Hoover, J. Edgar (1895–1972): director of the Federal Bureau of Investigation (FBI) from 1935 until his death; regarded as a pillar of probity and a staunch anti-Communist; after his death, questions were raised about his conduct as FBI director.

Hope, Bob (1903–): comedian, born in England as Leslie Townes Hope; specializes in rapid-fire monologue, a series of quick quips on any number of current subjects and personalities; beloved for his many trips overseas to entertain the troops; appeared in numerous movies, delighting audiences with his *Road* films.

Houdini, Harry (Erich Weiss) (1874–1926): born Erik Weisz in Hungary; the greatest of all escapologists, extricating himself from handcuffs, chained trunks, straitjackets, jails, water tanks, and paddy wagons; in later life devoted himself to debunking spiritualists.

Hurley, Cornelius "Connie" (1896–1976): colorful gambler, Los Angeles restaurateur, and Las Vegas shareholder in the Flamingo and Fremont Hotels.

Hurley's Horse Room: Hollywood; bookmaking establishment located next to the Brown Derby.

Hutton, Betty (1921–): actress, singer; made the big time as a vocalist with the Vincent Lopez Band; known as the "Blonde Bombshell"; went from Broadway to Hollywood, where she appeared in *Annie Get Your Gun* (1950).

Hyers, Frankie (?–1973): comedian; played nightclubs, particularly Club 18 in New York; engaged in ad-libbing, customer-baiting humor, made all the more frenetic by hecklers.

Inter-Ocean Hotel: Chicago; located at State and Van Buren Streets; a typical theatrical rooming house, with the lobby walls covered with photographs of vaudeville acts.

Irish Sweepstakes: called the *Sweeps;* based on the Manchester Handicap Horse Race; world's largest lottery, with proceeds split between winning ticket holders and Irish hospitals; replaced in the mid-1980s by a national lottery.

James, Freddie: See **Allen, Fred**.

Janis, Elsie (1889–1956): mimic, revue artist, author, songwriter; noted for her remarkable imitations; performed in one of the first one-woman shows on the legitimate stage; later wrote screenplays, songs, and books.

Jazz Singer, The (1927): called the "first talking film"; includes only a few passages of dialogue and some songs.

Jessel, George (1898–1981): entertainer, actor, songwriter, producer; appeared in vaudeville and silent films; in radio and television earned a reputation as an entertainer and songwriter; in the late 1940s and early 1950s produced musical films for Fox.

Joe Frisco dance: a jazz dance dating from 1917; "Joe Frisco, working in a tuxedo, derby, and cigar, introduced it at Chicago's Green Mill Garden. When [he] danced it at Rector's in New York that year, it had already become so famous that he was billed as 'Creator of the Jazz Dance'" (Green and Laurie, 1951).

John the Baptist: a first-century Jewish religious reformer; arrested by Herod and

GLOSSARY

beheaded because of his denunciation of Herod's marriage to Herodias: "It is not lawful for thee to have thy brother's wife" (Mark 6:18); Herodias counseled Salome, her daughter, to ask for John's head as a gift for her dance.

John's Rendezvous Restaurant: San Francisco; located at 50 Osgood Place, a narrow street south of Broadway, between Sansome and Montgomery; proprietors, John and W. J. Sobrato.

Jolson, Al (1886–1950): singer, actor, entertainer; as a child, he sang in synagogues, a circus, cafes, and vaudeville; rose to stardom on the New York stage before going into films; starred in the world's first talkie feature, *The Jazz Singer* (1927).

Katleman, Jake (1902–1950): hotelier; influential in gambling business in Palm Springs, California; later became manager and principal owner of El Rancho Vegas.

Kedzie Theatre: Chicago; located until 1932 at 3202 West Madison; then moved to 3210 West Madison; opened 1910, playing vaudeville and stock companies; later became a movie house.

Keith, B[enjamin] F[ranklin] (1846–1914): owner of the vast Keith theatre chain; said to have started and maintained vaudeville; with his general manager, E. F. Albee, he controlled virtually every vaudeville act in America.

Keith's Chestnut Street Theatre: Philadelphia; located at 1116 Chestnut Street between Eleventh and Twelfth; opened Saturday, November 8, 1902; the city's first million-dollar theatre; decorated palatially, with delicate murals, framed damasks, marble sculptures, crystal chandeliers, and plush rugs.

Keith's Colonial Theatre: New York; located on Broadway between Sixty-second and Sixty-third Streets; famous for its unruly gallery crowds, who would clap their hands in unison or throw pennies at the performer when they didn't care for an act; now the site of the Atrium apartment building.

Keith's Palace Theatre: New York; located at 1564 Broadway between Forty-sixth and Forty-seventh Streets, on the northeast corner of Broadway and Forty-seventh Street; opened as a vaudeville theatre on March 24, 1913; known as the Valhalla of Vaudeville; every variety artist yearned to play the Palace.

Keith's Theatre News: published in New York from 1928 to 1932.

Kelly, Gene (1912–1996): dancer, actor, choreographer, director; danced on Broadway in *Leave It to Me* (1938); choreographed "Billy Rose's Diamond Horseshoe"; in films, succeeded Fred Astaire as Hollywood's dancing master and revolutionized Hollywood musicals with his dance routines.

Kentucky Derby: Louisville, Kentucky; originated in 1875 as a mirror of England's famed Epsom Derby; run on the first Saturday in May; the first race in Thoroughbreds' Triple Crown; called "the greatest two minutes in sports."

Kirk, Joe (1904?–1975): comedian; a vaudevillian who played all the top houses, including the Palace; a longtime associate of the deadpan mime and comedian Ben Blue (1901–1975).

Klee, Mel (1893–1935): vaudevillian; started as a song plugger; became a standard single in both white- and blackface; later was frequently the headliner for Fanchon and Marco Ideas and appeared with other girl acts.

LaHiff, Billy (1883?–1934): restaurateur noted for his generosity to financially distressed actors; owned the Tavern, a chop house on West Forty-eighth Street and a rendezvous for Broadway professionals and film stars.

Lambs' Club: started in 1874; the first actors' club in America; prior to 1905, the club frequently changed locations; after 1905, located at 130 West Forty-fourth Street, where the club became famous; performed for its members sketches called Gambols, some of which became Broadway hits.

Lancashire clog: a type of clog dance, popular with vaudeville audiences, featuring triples, rolls, and nerve steps; the dancer, confined to jigging in one spot, is judged according to time, style, beat, and execution.

Lehr, Lew (1895–1950): comedian, gag writer, producer, newsreel executive of Fox Movietone News; performed a zany dialect comedy and numerous accents; well known for his newsreel comedy and his line, "Monkeys is the cwaziest people."

Lewis, Joe E. (1901–1971): nightclub comedian and sometime singer; called Peck's Bad Boy of the Nightclubs for his off-color jokes about "booze, broads, and bang tails [horses]"; one of the most beloved entertainers, owing to his generosity.

Lichtman, Al (1888–1958): motion picture pioneer, one of the earliest distributors, producer; figured prominently in the launching of CinemaScope; closed deal for release of *Gone with the Wind;* a Metro-Goldwyn-Mayer executive.

Lloyd, Harold (1893–1971): silent film comedian; first created the popular character of Lonesome Luke; then created the Everyman character that became his trademark and vehicle to success; in the 1920s, his films outdrew Chaplin's and Keaton's.

London Shop: Los Angeles; located at 5621 Hollywood Boulevard; fashionable store originally called the London Gift Shop.

Lone Palm (motel): Palm Springs; located at 1276 North Indian Avenue, now called Indian Canyon Avenue.

Longden, Johnny (1907–): jockey; rode more than six thousand winners in forty years; in 1943, riding Citation, won the Kentucky Derby, the Preakness, and the Belmont Stakes; in 1956 elected to the jockeys' Hall of Fame; retired 1966.

Louisiana Lo-Downs: no information available.

GLOSSARY

Lum and Abner: a fifteen-minute comedy radio program about Lum Edwards (Chester Lauck) and Abner Peabody (Norris Goff), "fellers from the hills"; set in the fictional town of Pine Ridge, Arkansas, the skits effectively mixed hillbilly humor and soap opera; ran from 1931 to 1953.

Lyman, Abe (1897–1957): drummer, bandleader, songwriter; hit the big time when his band played the Cocoanut Grove in Hollywood for five years, a record for the spot; appeared not only in nightclubs but also in films and on radio.

Lyric Theatre: New York; located at 213 West Forty-second Street; opened on October 12, 1903; built to be the home of the American School of Opera; for a number of years, musical theatre alternated with drama, until the Depression, when it became a movie theatre.

Mack, Roy (1892–1962): short subjects director for Warner Brothers in New York before going to Hollywood in the 1930s.

McCarthy, Neil S. (1888?–1972): sportsman-lawyer and former Howard Hughes empire executive; clients included Louis B. Mayer, Cecil B. De Mille, and Paramount Pictures.

McDermott, Loretta (?): reportedly a small, slim, beautiful woman; she and Frisco appeared initially in a ballroom dancing act billed as "Francisco and Loretta," an act credited with introducing dinner dancing to New Orleans and Chicago. "They would do their act. Then Loretta would ask some gentleman to dance with her, and Frisco would ask a lady to dance with him" (Holbrook, 1976).

Machpelah Cemetery: Ridgewood, New York; located at 82-30 Cypress Hills Street.

Majestic Theatre: Chicago; located at 18 West Monroe between State and Dearborn; the first million-dollar theatre (it was also a twenty-two-story office building); built by the Lehman estate, owners of the Fair department store; opened January 1, 1906; renamed Shubert in 1945.

Marx, Chico (1886–1961): born Leonard Marx; comic actor; one of the Marx brothers; played the role of a larcenous Italian who spoke with an impossible accent that caused endless comic misunderstandings; started in vaudeville and performed in films.

Marx, Groucho (1890–1977): born Julius Marx; a zany comedian, writer; noted for his anarchical humor and characteristic slouch, black-smudged mustache, long cigar, and leer; famous films include *Duck Soup* (1933) and *A Night at the Opera* (1935); for fourteen years emceed television's "You Bet Your Life."

Marx, Harpo (1893–1964): born Adolph Marx; one of the Marx brothers; stage name came from his fondness for playing the harp; wore a curly, unruly wig and acted the part of a mute who communicated with the others by means of honks, whistles, and pantomimic gestures that only Chico could interpret.

Masquers Club: founded May 12, 1925, in Hollywood as a fraternal organization for show business people; motto, "We Laugh to Win"; through the years produced *Revels,* two-reel comedies, and plays.

Mayer, Louis B. (1885–1957): as a young man owned a chain of movie theatres; in 1917 formed his own production company; in 1924 appointed vice president and general manager of Metro-Goldwyn-Mayer; helped build MGM into one of the great studios.

Meakin, Walter (1870?–1931): vaudeville agent and manager who booked a small circuit of out-of-town theatres.

Merman, Ethel (1909–1984): musical comedy singer and actress; first performed in cabaret and vaudeville; played in numerous Broadway hit musical shows; won the New York Drama Critics Award for her performance of Rose in *Gypsy* (1959).

Midnight Frolic: New York; located atop the New Amsterdam Theatre; inaugurated by Ziegfeld in January 1915; "a sumptuous cabaret, serving superb food, dancing, and elaborate chorus girl productions to the best of the carriage trade . . . a model of revue entertainment" (Erenberg, 1981).

Mioland (born 1937): racehorse; ran second to Bay View in the 1941 Santa Anita Handicap; won American Derby at Washington Park (1940), San Juan Capistrano Handicap (1940 and 1941), San Pasqual Handicap, and San Antonio Handicap (1941).

Moran, Polly (1884–1952): loudmouthed, buck-toothed comic star and character comedienne of numerous silent and sound films; often co-starred with the comedic character actress Marie Dressler (1869–1934); started in vaudeville.

Mosconi, Lou (1895–1969): a dancer; performed in vaudeville and musical comedy with his brother Charles Jr. and his sister Verna; after retiring from the stage, ran a dance school in Los Angeles; set a show business record by playing the Palace on Broadway fifty-two weeks over a period of seven seasons.

Motion Picture Country Home (now called the Motion Picture and Television Fund Retirement Home): Woodland Hills (Los Angeles); then and now located at 23388 Mulholland Drive.

Murray, Mae (1885–1965): actress; began as a child dancer; appeared on Broadway in several editions of Ziegfeld *Follies;* recruited for silent films because of her beautiful face ("The Girl with the Bee-Stung Lips"), but did not fare well in talkies.

Musso and Frank Grill: Los Angeles; located at 6667 Hollywood Boulevard; familiarly called Musso Frank's; a popular restaurant.

Nemo Theatre: New Orleans; located at 322 Opelousas Avenue, between Bouny and Powder Streets; offered vaudeville and movies; the Nemo later became the

GLOSSARY

Avenue Academy, popular for dances, style shows, and meetings.

New Amsterdam Theatre: New York; located at 214–216 West Forty-second Street, west of Seventh Avenue; opened November 2, 1903; home of Florenz Ziegfeld's *Follies* every year, except from 1913 to 1927; now owned by Disney, which converted it from a cinema back to a theatre.

Nick the Greek (Nicholas Andrea Dandolos) (1886–1966): gambler; noted for his love of gambling, which he plied in Las Vegas and Monte Carlo and in furtive games in small hotel rooms; born in Crete.

Nijinsky, Vaslav (1890–1950): world-famous Russian ballet dancer and choreographer; regarded as the finest male dancer in the history of ballet; scandalized the dancing world with his daring choreography.

Norworth, Jack (1879–1959): composer; vaudeville and musical comedy performer; wrote "Take Me Out to the Ball Game" and "Shine on Harvest Moon"; performed also in radio, television, and films.

Orpheum Circuit: the major vaudeville circuit for the West Coast and part of the Midwest; at the height of its popularity in the 1920s, the Orpheum Circuit, Inc., owned outright over forty theatres in the United States and Canada and had financial interests in hundreds of others.

Orpheum Theatre: Los Angeles; then and now located at 842 Broadway.

Orpheum Theatre: San Francisco; then and now located at 1192 Market Street.

Palace Theatre: Chicago; located at Randolph and La Salle; replaced the old Palace Music Hall; opened October 4, 1926; interior, with six varieties of imported marble, modeled after the palaces of Fontainebleau and Versailles; had five grand lobbies and foyers and artworks from the Vanderbilt estate.

Palace Theatre (New York): See **Keith's Palace Theatre**.

Palmer House: Chicago; located at 17 East Monroe, near State Street; opened 1875; for many years considered Chicago's best hotel, with its lavish interiors of marble, imported woods, mosaics, frescoes, and other embellishments.

Palooka, Joe: a popular comic strip that first appeared in 1928; the hero, an unsophisticated and naively honest prize fighter, was known for his fair play, love of mother and home, and patriotism.

Pantages Theatre: Hollywood; then and now located at 6233 Hollywood Boulevard.

Parkyakarkus (Harry Einstein) (1904–1958): comedian; went from stage to radio to films; a popular comic in the 1930s on the Eddie Cantor radio show; died onstage.

Pearl, Jack (1894–1984): comedian; appeared on radio as Baron Munchausen, known for his famous line: "Vass you dere, Sharlie?"

"Peck's Bad Boy [and His Pa]": a short story by George Wilbur Peck (1840–1916).

Pepper, Jack (1903?–1979): comedian; started in vaudeville with his sisters; played on Broadway for the Shuberts and Ziegfeld; had a radio show and then became a nightclub owner; appeared in Hope and Crosby *Road* films.

Perino's Restaurant: Los Angeles; located in the 1930s at 3927 Wilshire Boulevard, by the early 1950s at 4101 Wilshire Boulevard.

Pickford, Mary (1893–1979): actress; as a child actor toured with various road companies; at fourteen starred in a Broadway play; in the heyday of silent films known as "America's Sweetheart"; cofounder of United Artists Films; Academy Award winner.

Pierson, Newbold L. (1917–1965): jockey; associated with the great Calumet Farm; called a "money rider"; finished second in the 1948 Kentucky Derby riding Coaltown (Citation won).

Pink Poodle Cafe: New Orleans; no information available; there was, however, a *Poodle Dog Cafe* (circa 1908–1917) located at Liberty and Bienville Streets, where Buddy Petit's band played.

Pinza, Ezio (1892–1957): the great Metropolitan Opera basso who appeared on Broadway in *South Pacific,* charming audiences with his singing of "Some Enchanted Evening."

Plaza Hotel: Hollywood; located at 1637 North Vine Street.

Portnoy, Frank S. (1887–1985): a longtime hotel host in Las Vegas.

Powell, Eleanor (1912–1982): dancer, actress; reached Broadway at seventeen and Hollywood at twenty-three; tap danced through films until the mid-1940s, when her popularity declined.

Price, George (1900–1964): comedian, impressionist, song-and-dance man; started in vaudeville with Gus Edwards's *School Days;* played Broadway and toured cafes; noted for his rendition of "Bye Bye Blackbird."

Rabwin, Marcus (1901–1988): surgeon, scholar; studied at the University of Minnesota and in Vienna; senior surgeon at Cedars of Lebanon; authored the book *X-Ray Diagnosis of Intestinal Obstruction* (1930); maintained an office in Beverly Hills at 9730 Wilshire Boulevard.

Racing Form: See **Daily Racing Form.**

Raft, George (1895–1980): actor; began as a prizefighter, then became a ballroom dancer before moving on to nightclubs and Broadway; in the late 1920s went to Hollywood and was cast as a Valentino-type; later moved on to gangster roles; owned gambling clubs and moved in mob circles.

Rambova, Natasha (Winifred Shaunessy) (1897–1966): actress, set designer, dance teacher, Egyptologist; second wife of Valentino; took charge of Valentino's

GLOSSARY

career and badly advised him to become less manly and more effeminate; offended studio executives, who banned her from the set.

Rasputin, Harry (Victor Weinshenker) (1889–1957): Chicago press agent, bon vivant, go-between, nightclubber, theatre-goer, stage-door-Johnny; loved show business and especially Yiddish theatre; publicist for Louis Armstrong and Billy Daniels; accompanied Armstrong on several European tours.

Raye, Martha (1916–1994): wide-mouthed, boisterous comedienne and vocalist; played burlesque, nightclubs, films, and television; greatest success came on Broadway in *Hello Dolly* (1967) and *No, No Nanette* revival (1972).

Rector's Tavern: New York; located at Broadway (no. 1506) and Forty-fourth Street; described by Theodore Dreiser in *Sister Carrie* as a dining place with "polished marble walls and floors, [a] profusion of lights, [a] show of china and silverware, and above all, [a] reputation as a resort for actors and professional men."

Rendezvous: Miami or Miami Beach; no information available.

Resista: no information about her is available; the act, like that of Johnny Coulon and Annie Abbott, was long popular in vaudeville: the performer defied anyone in the audience to lift him or her off the stage.

Rhodes, "Little" Billy (1895–1967): actor; in his day, the best known midget in Hollywood; started on Broadway stage with Ziegfeld and George M. Cohan; appeared in *Wizard of Oz* and other films.

Richards, Cully (1908–1978): comedian, character actor, writer; started in vaudeville, then moved on to films; wrote and performed for Jackie Gleason's variety show during the 1960s; a half-owner of Slapsie Maxie's restaurant.

Richman, Harry (1895–1972): a song-and-dance man and songwriter; performed with top hat or straw hat, tails, and cane; reveled in being a lady's man.

Ritz, Al (1901–1965): dancer, comedian; eldest of the Ritz brothers; performed with brothers Jimmy and Harry; began as a dancer—tap, challenge, acrobatic, and unison—but gradually added comedy, chiefly of the mugging and knockabout sort.

Ritz Brothers: Al (see above), Jimmy (1903–1985), and the leader, Harry (1906–1986): combined zany, slapstick, and acrobatic comedy; rowdy and robust clowning, dancing, and singing; performed in nightclubs, musicals, films, and television.

Roberts, Benny (?): known throughout the profession simply as "Benny"; started as a violinist in Keith's Union Square theatre; from 1903 on, conducted in New York for every major vaudeville act; considered one of the great musical conductors of vaudeville; played the Palace, the old Alhambra, and other famous houses.

Robinson, Bill "Bojangles" (1878–1949): tap dancer, actor, entertainer; famous for his stairway dance; played vaudeville, musical stage, and films; best remembered for his movie appearances with Shirley Temple.

Rockefeller, John D[avison] (1839–1937): industrialist and philanthropist; created the modern petroleum industry; pioneered large-scale philanthropy, giving millions to education and medical sciences; often called the richest man in the world—and a robber baron.

Rogers, Will (1879–1935): rider, rope twirler, humorist, columnist; famous for his homespun philosophy; roving ambassador and spokesman for rural America; became popular on radio and in the press for his political opinions.

Roof Garden: See **Midnight Frolic** and **New Amsterdam Theatre**.

Rooney, Pat, Sr. (1844–1892): song-and-dance man; born in Birmingham, England; humanized his Irish comic characterizations; dressed in incongruous clothes—for example, a cutaway coat and fancy waistcoat with pants sporting large plaid checks—he would dance and sing favorites, like "Biddy the Ballet Girl."

Rooney, Pat, Jr. (1880–1962): dancer, singer, songwriter; performed with his wife, Marion Bent, in musical comedies and revues; a frequent guest on the Ed Sullivan show; famous for his dance routine, "She's the Daughter of Rosie O'Grady," in which he kept his hands in his pockets while performing a clog dance.

Roosevelt, Theodore "Teddy" (1858–1919): twenty-sixth president of the United States, from 1901 to 1909; nationalist, reformer, labor sympathizer, friend of the poor and destitute; convinced that morality was the measure of manliness; loved the outdoors—hunting, fishing, trekking, camping.

Rosenbloom, Maxie (Slapsie) (1903–1976): prizefighter and comic actor; light-heavyweight champion in the early 1930s; appeared in a number of films from the 1930s to the 1960s, usually playing a punch-drunk Damon Runyon–type character.

Rothstein, Bill: no information available.

Runyon, Damon (1884–1946): journalist, sportswriter, screenwriter, author, producer; developed an individual style called Runyonese that lovingly chronicled the amusing behavior of guys and dolls who employ a streetwise, colorful Broadway slang.

Saint Patrick's Cathedral: New York; located on Fifth Avenue between Fiftieth and Fifty-first.

Sans Souci (restaurant): Chicago; located at 6000 Cottage Grove, Hyde Park.

Santa Anita Racetrack: Arcadia, California; opened Christmas Day, 1934; pioneered the hundred-thousand-dollar purse and electric timing, with times posted for public viewing (1935); European-style turf course (built 1953) rated one of the best in North America; the most successful thoroughbred track in the country.

Schindler's Theatre: Chicago; located at 1009 West Huron; seated 953; opened 1913, closed 1954; presumably called Schindler's "castle" because it was part of the Kohl and Castle Midwest theatre circuit; the theatre was named after Ludwig Schindler, whose last name is incorrectly spelled Shindler in a number of vaud histories.

Scratch Sheet: a daily publication listing the horses and jockeys racing that day, with a prediction of the odds on each horse, and a number for each horse that bettors use for placing a bet with a bookie.

Sedley, Roy (?): dancer, comedian, monologist; noted for his pants-falling act and his trigger-fast ad-libbing and baiting of customers; appeared in Broadway musical *Hot-Cha!* (1932); played nightclubs, especially Club 18, and acted as master of ceremonies at parties.

Seven Little Foys: See **Foy, Eddie, Sr.**

Sherman House: Chicago; located at North Clark and West Randolph; opened 1904, closed 1973; said to have the longest bar in the world; associated with Democratic party politicians because they frequently stayed there; a favorite spot of Chicago's smart set.

Shore, Sylvia (?): singer, dancer, comedienne; satirized different types of formal dancing; noted for her acrobatics and loose-jointed antics; appeared in George White's *New 1941 Scandals Cavalcade* at Loew's State Theatre (New York).

Silverman, Sime (1873–1933): founder and editor of *Variety;* prided himself on his theatrical journalism, which totally ignored advertisers' feelings; its distinctive style appealed to newsmen, with its slang, tempo, unconventional grammar, inversion of nouns to read as verbs, and abbreviations.

Sinatra, Frank (1915–1998): singer, actor; started singing on radio, in nightclubs, and for bands; became the rage of teenagers, who called him "the Voice"; initially appeared in light musical films; later won acclaim in serious film roles, leading to an Academy Award.

Smith, Joe (Charles Marks) (1884–1981): comedian; teamed with Charles Dale in "Dr. Kronkhite" skit, a comedy routine famous for its wit and timing; appeared in films with Dale (for example, *The Heart of New York*); the two men provided the model for Neil Simon's *The Sunshine Boys.*

Smith, William J. (1901–1984): Hollywood agent for Feldman-Blum; publicist for Twentieth Century-Fox studio; married Ethel Merman November 16, 1940; she divorced him less than a year later.

Somerset Hotel: New York; located at 150 West Forty-seventh Street.

Starr, Jimmie (1904?–1990): columnist, screenwriter, and novelist; in 1924 pioneered the Hollywood movie newspaper column, writing gossip and reviews for the *Los Angeles Daily Record;* later moved to the *Los Angeles Express,* subsequently called the *Los Angeles Herald Express.*

Strand Theatre: Battle Creek, Michigan; located at 14 Main East; opened August 14, 1915, as city's finest, with tapestries, leather and plush seats, mahogany woodwork, gold trimmings, velvet rugs, and a Kimball pipe organ.

Summerville, George "Slim" (1892–1946): comedian, actor, director; became famous as one of Mack Sennett's Keystone Cops; lanky and mournful, he personified rural America; later served as a director and gagman for Sennett.

Sweet Sixteen Bathing Beauties: probably produced by Joe Hart, whose "Bathing Girls" acts were very popular; "to break up the monotony of watching singles, doubles, trios, and quartets . . . vaudeville used what was called 'big acts' or 'girl acts' for a 'flash' of bigness on the show" (Laurie, 1953).

Tanguay, Eva (1878–1947): singer, dancer, frenetic personality considered by some to be the preeminent figure in vaudeville; began her fabulous, colorful career in an unlikely manner, by advertising herself in newspapers; famous for her singing of "I Don't Care."

Tannen, Julius (1881–1965): monologist, columnist, character actor; started in vaudeville, moved on to Broadway, films, and television; a cerebral comic, breaking off a joke just before the climax, leaving the punch line to the audience; credited with pioneering the stand-up comedian style.

Texas Tommy dance: said to be the first African American dance accepted by whites; traced to a black cabaret on the Barbary Coast of San Francisco; arrived in New York (1910) from Chicago; a shimmying jazz dance that makes up in suggestive and violent shaking movements what it lacks in subtlety.

Thin Man, The (1934): a film based on Dashiell Hammett's crime novel; Nick Charles, the detective, was played by William Powell and Nora Charles, his wife, by Myrna Loy.

Thorek, Dr. Max (1880–1960): born in Hungary; practiced in Chicago, principally as a plastic surgeon; wrote numerous medical books; founded the American Hospital in Chicago, renamed in 1975 the Thorek Hospital, in honor of its founder.

Tibbett, Lawrence (1896–1960): operatic baritone; sang with the Metropolitan Opera for twenty-eight years; in the early 1930s starred in a number of musical films.

Tin Pan Alley: originally the name given to a district in New York (Twenty-eighth Street between Fifth Avenue and Broadway) where many songwriters, arrangers, and music publishers were located; the name became synonymous with the American popular music industry from the late 1880s until the middle of the twentieth century.

GLOSSARY

Toto the Clown (Armando "Toto" Novello) (1888–1938): comic clown; at one time the highest paid clown in America; wore grotesque makeup, performed various contortions, and always made "his entrance in a toy car that was far too small for him, let alone his dog, Whiskey, who came along for the ride" (Slide, 1994).

Triplicate (born 1941): racehorse; owned by Fred Astaire; won the Hollywood Gold Cup at Hollywood Park (1946), the San Juan Capistrano at Santa Anita (1946), and the Golden Gate Handicap at Golden Gate Fields, California (1947).

Tucker, Sophie (1884–1966): singer; the heavyweight "red hot mamma" of vaudeville owing to her risqué songs and repartee, which blended energy and movement with sentiment and sex; formed her own combo to back her up (1917–1921); her trademark song was "Some of These Days"; appeared in numerous films.

Unique Theatre: Staples, Minnesota; located at corner of Second Avenue and Fifth Street; active 1914–1927; after 1927, name was changed to Grand Theatre, when emphasis shifted from vaudeville to movies.

Valentino, Rudolph (1895–1926): dancer, silent film actor; the great romantic idol of the 1920s; died suddenly from a perforated ulcer, causing several suicides; his funeral became a national event; began as a taxi driver.

Van Buren, Grace: no information available.

Variety: New York; the leading American entertainment trade paper; begun in 1905, it was admired for its uncompromisingly honest reviews; still published weekly; known as the "Bible of Show Business"; see **Silverman, Sime.**

Verdi Theatre: Chicago; located at 2035 West Thirty-fifth Street; opened 1904.

Victoria Theatre: four theatres in Chicago: (1) 2811 West Cermak, opened 1908; (2) 3131 West Logan Boulevard, opened 1918; (3) 10936 South Michigan, opened 1904; (4) 3143 North Sheffield, opened 1911, later known as Vic, German, and Old Vic (this is probably the theatre Frisco played).

Walker, Buddy (1898?–1979): singer; started out as a member of Gus Edwards's *School Days* act; later worked as a social director in resorts and Miami hotels.

Wall, Nick (1909–1983): jockey; a "money rider"; one of the greatest lightweight riders of all time (weighed less than a hundred pounds with a regulation saddle); in 1938 won the Santa Anita handicap and ended the year the leading money winner.

Western Union (telegraph company): established in 1851; completed the first transcontinental telegraph line; by 1900 had a million miles of lines and two international cables; synonymous with telegram service.

Westrope, Jack "Jackie" (1918?–1958): jockey; started racing as a kid; won the national riding championship at fifteen; died when thrown from a horse during the running of the Hollywood Oaks at Hollywood Park; rode more than twenty-four hundred winners.

Wheeler, Bert (1895–1968): comedian; started as a child performer; in his early twenties became a vaudeville comedy headliner; played in Ziegfeld *Follies;* in 1927 teamed with Robert Woolsey.

White, Jack (1899?–1984): writer, producer, director; started as a child actor opposite Charlie Chaplin and Gloria Swanson; directed at RKO; for many years wrote, produced, and directed "Three Stooges" films.

Whiting, Margaret (1924–): singer; worked with Johnny Mercer, Freddie Slack, Paul Whiteman; her father, Richard Whiting (1891–1938), wrote music for Broadway musicals and films; a number of his songs became major hits.

Winchell, Walter (1897–1972): columnist, newscaster; chronicled the affairs of the high and mighty; syndicated in some one thousand papers; the undisputed "Boswell" of New York nightclubs; catapulted people and places into fame and fortune with his plugs.

Winning Wire: a southern California 1940s radio racing results program on station KRKD; lasted only a few years; for a fee, offered tips and specials; a tout service.

Woolsey, Robert (1889–1938): part of comedy team of Wheeler and Woolsey; Wheeler played the straight man and Woolsey, with his perennial cigar, the funnyman; together popularized the sort of "Who's on first" humor that Abbot and Costello made famous.

Wright, Jim: no information available.

Wynn, Ed (1886–1966): comedian; called "The Perfect Fool" (from 1921 musical); went from vaudeville to radio to films to television; never uttered an off-color joke; in the 1950s made films playing fey old gentlemen; in 1958 had his own television show.

Ziegfeld, Florenz "Flo" (1867–1932): Broadway impresario; probably the most publicized theatrical manager in American stage history; created the Ziegfeld *Follies,* patterned after the Parisian *Folies Bergère;* launched innumerable careers.

Zit (Carl F. Zittel) (1876–1943): journalist, publisher, entrepreneur; restaurateur; published *Zit's Theatrical Weekly,* more a gossip than a trade paper, famous for its grading sheet that rated vaudeville performers.

"Loretta, How Could You?"
An Essay on Chronology

ROBERTA C. MARTIN

The preceding record of Joe Frisco's career is perhaps even more anecdotal than most show business memoirs. Lowry's account of Frisco's life sketchily attempts a chronology, but the stories Lowry tells about Joe seem to float above that chronology like laugh lines over an empty stage. Although Lowry rarely mentions dates and places, it is possible to verify some of the important ones that ground Lowry's account. Others—a good number of them—prove more elusive, provoking the investigator to ask why. What were Ed Lowry's own narrative purposes, and how did they alter his view?[1]

It is important to acknowledge at the outset that one cause of the unreliable chronology is simply the sense of fun with which Lowry reports Joe's antic routines, comic remarks, and hilarious rejoinders. Like the stand-up comic that Lowry himself was, he often lets one story remind him of another to suggest the fecundity of Joe's wit. This associative process appears to depend on two mechanisms: First, one anecdote prompts another because it involves the same people or places; and second, stories are often grouped according to a broadly geographical periodization—first, events that occurred in the Midwest and in Chicago; then those that took place in New York and elsewhere on the East Coast; and finally, incidents from Joe's later years in Los Angeles and on the West Coast. Within this framework, we recognize some errors in both locality and chronology as ordinary memory lapses that might well happen to a seasoned vaudevillian gleefully recalling the comic genius of an old friend. Other errors result from the comedian's tendency to shape his material so that each chapter builds toward a punch line. Within any given chapter, what comes last is not necessarily what happened last, but what was funniest.

The episodic character of Lowry's story, however, partly conflicts with other, overarching narrative objectives, some purposeful and some perhaps unconscious. Clearly, Lowry wishes to organize the memoir chronologically, giving an account of Joe's life from its start in Milan, Illinois, to its conclusion in Hollywood. But he also needs to account for certain character traits that, although they provided the material for much of Joe's comic inventiveness, seem to Lowry to cry out for explanation.

Joe Frisco had problems. He was a heavy drinker and apparently a compulsive gambler who was beset by money troubles to the end of his life. Joe also seems to have endured significant periods of what we would today call severe depression. To account satisfactorily for Joe's constant emotional and monetary difficulties, Lowry's ostensibly straightforward chronology undergoes a subtle reorganization based on those relationships that he considers the major influences on Joe—relationships with his father, with his mother, and especially with Loretta McDermott, the woman whom Lowry seems almost single-handedly to construct as the "love of Joe's life."

There exists no independent evidence that Joe's relationship with Loretta was as central to his life as Lowry asserts or that their attachment lasted as long as Lowry implies. In fact, several major chronological dislocations identifiable from narrative materials within the text and from scant external sources suggest that the arrangement of episodes involving Loretta—as well as some involving Joe's mother—creates a "false chronology." The effect of this rearrangement is to blame Joe's drinking and his gambling on his relationship with Loretta and, to a lesser extent, on his relationship with his mother and his guilt over his father's death.

Lowry's desire to blame Joe's destructive habits and emotional turmoil largely on Loretta leads him to introduce her into events and situations in which the surrounding narrative material suggests dates five or even ten years after their actual relationship ended. This impulse is especially evident in the episodes occurring during the 1920s, when Lowry's concern over Joe's character leads him to juxtapose events concerning Loretta and those involving Joe's mother. Once Lowry has inflated Loretta's effect on Joe, he must then extend her influence on him into his later, even sadder years. The result is a confusion over Joe's last contacts with Loretta—did they occur in 1943, in 1950, or as late as 1956?

Lowry may have had another, only dimly perceived, reason for his romance chronology. By foregrounding a partly invented love interest for Joe, Lowry deflects attention from the fact that, by his own account, the closest and most enduring relationship in Joe's adult life was with Charlie Foy—a friendship that Lowry clearly fears might, in the absence of a heterosexual love interest, arouse speculation about Joe's sexuality.[2]

The portrait of Joe Frisco that emerges from Lowry's shaping of his materials is of an archetypal vaudevillian—a comic genius who is nevertheless the tragic clown haunted by the memory of his lost love, anguished over his senile mother, and, in the fading days of vaudeville, persecuted by the IRS, which takes over as the villain of the piece when neither Loretta nor Joe's mother can plausibly continue to fill that role. While we may be skeptical of Lowry's attempt to blame others for Joe's problems, Lowry saves his account from becoming a melodrama by letting Joe's comedic brilliance speak for itself. Despite narrational distortions, Lowry's anecdotal strategy makes clear the one indisputable fact about Joe—he was a very funny guy.

Joe was born Louis W. Joseph in Milan, Illinois, near Rock Island. *The Oxford Companion to American Theatre* gives Joe Frisco's birth date tentatively as 1890. It is probably more accurate, however, to assume a date sometime in the early or mid 1890s because the one fairly firm date we have for Joe's early days in Milan is 1912 or 1913, when as a teenager he probably saw Eddie Foy in *Over the River*.[3] Lowry's description of Joe's reaction to that performance, like his account of Joe's quarrel with his father and his running away from home, suggests a teenage boy rather than a young man in his early twenties. This reference undermines the claim made in the *New York Times* obituary that Joe went to Chicago in 1906. A better date for Joe's arrival in Chicago is approximately 1913. He probably saw Fred Allen (then performing as Freddy Saint James) when Allen played the Majestic (not exclusively the Great Northern, also known as the Hippodrome) from about 1915 to 1916. Joe would then have been in his late teens or early twenties. This period may also have been about the time Joe met Loretta McDermott.

We can begin sorting out the vexed issues of chronology that surround the length of Joe's relationship to Loretta McDermott by noting that it is possible that Gus Edwards's "advances" toward Loretta occurred several years before she met Joe, when she was still a teenager, and that the *Song*

Review (one of Edwards's many) in which Loretta had a very slight part was the one that debuted on October 3, 1914. Joe would then have met her in late 1914 or early 1915 and formed a partnership with her. It is also probable that Joe found the willing agent "who had not seen their act" around 1915–1917. The various adventures the couple had together as unknown entertainers most likely took place between 1914 and 1916.

Independent evidence suggests that Joe and Loretta's vaudeville circuit travels with Bill "Bojangles" Robinson probably occurred in about 1916 or 1917, after Robinson had split up with his partner, George W. Cooper, and had been "allowed" to become a "single" headliner and not part of a "colored pair."[4] Joe, Loretta, and Robinson seem to have traveled the Butterfield Circuit, which dominated the entire Midwest except Chicago. At the conclusion of this run of engagements, Joe came back to Chicago, according to Lowry, "a much more seasoned trouper and showman" who wanted to combine his act with the "Dixieland Five."[5]

At this point, Lowry's chronology raises serious questions. They center on the death of Joe's father, his breakup with Loretta, and the time and place of Joe's rise to fame as a "jazz dancer." Lowry's chapter "Jazz via New Orleans" suggests that Joe's famous "jazz dance" became popular while Joe and Loretta were still unknowns performing in the Midwest and the South. Moreover, Lowry's chapter "Goodbye, Poppa" suggests that both the death of Joe's father and the breakup with Loretta likewise occurred before Joe left Chicago for New York in 1917. The 1916 issues of the *Chicago Tribune,* however, contain no evidence that the jazz dance had caught on with audiences there. And the *Variety* obituary on Joe, which calls his dance the "Jewish Charleston," reports that he introduced it at the Palace in New York in 1926.

Lowry connects Joe's absence from Chicago at the time of his father's death with Loretta's "betrayal" of Joe and his sudden departure for New York in 1917. This story is dramatic but problematic. Lowry's account puts Joe in Chicago performing in Mike Fritzel's cafe at the time of his father's death. But Lowry also reports this death as occurring at about the same time as the death of Joe's brother. And *Variety* reports that Joe canceled his engagement at the Palace in New York in September 1927 to go to Missouri for his brother's funeral.[6]

Furthermore, a *Variety* review of Joe and Loretta in New York on October 24, 1918, as well as other evidence, indicates that Joe and Loretta were still together—or back together—in New York at various times during 1918 and 1919. We can be fairly sure that after 1917 Joe divided his time among New York, Chicago, and the various Midwestern and Southern circuits. Lowry's account probably conflates many journeys back and forth between Chicago, where Joe was apparently a familiar figure, and New York, the scene of his greatest success. The Fritzel episodes probably belong to this period.

In short, the whole romance-bereavement-betrayal-departure sequence could not have been as causally neat as Lowry presents it. We have no external evidence to confirm Lowry's assertion that Joe departed for New York in response to Loretta's first betrayal, but if he did, this event obviously could not have occurred at the time of his brother's or his father's death. It is most likely that the betrayal, Joe's departure for New York, and the deaths were separate episodes that Lowry draws together in his narrative to rationalize Joe's emotional difficulties.

The "My Broadway" chapter of Lowry's account, whose ostensible purpose is to describe Joe's rise as a popular vaudeville star, is crucial to Lowry's attempt to "explain" Joe's character. It encompasses the entire period from Joe's appearance in Florenz Ziegfeld's *Follies* in 1918 to about 1929–1930, when he went to Los Angeles for the filming of *The Gorilla*. When Joe joins the cast of the 1918 *Follies*, we are once again on firm chronological ground. But Lowry's account of Joe's appearance with Ziegfeld is intertwined with the ongoing Joe and Loretta romance in such a way that it is hard to determine just how long Joe actually stayed with the *Follies*. His edition of the *Follies* opened in Atlantic City around June 12, 1918, and premiered in New York at the New Amsterdam Roof on June 14, 1918. It ended its run at the New Amsterdam Roof on September 14, 1918, and apparently was scheduled to open at the Globe in New York on October 7, but no *Variety* review of such a performance appears. The show then began a road tour and played in Boston on October 4.[7] The evidence, however, suggests that Joe was not part of the *Follies* road tour.

The *Follies* run during this year is difficult to trace because an epidemic of Spanish influenza stopped all shows in the area, and the various acts in most shows scattered during the course of the epidemic to pick up work where they could. The medical ban was lifted in Boston on October 19. *Variety* reports that "Frisco and Jazz Band (Harry Weber)" opened as a "new act" in New York around October 11, 1918, and "Frisco and Band" played Proctor's in Newark, New Jersey, on October 14, 1918. The *Follies* opened as a "new act" at Proctor's in New York during the week of October 25, 1918, but Joe was not with the show then nor was he with the show after November 5.

From this point forward in Lowry's history, the various episodes are arranged according to Lowry's sense of their appropriateness as indications of Joe's character, and the suggestion of a chronology operates merely as a narrative device that lends coherence to the incidents. For example, the story at the beginning of the "My Broadway" chapter about Joe at the Friar's Club, occurring as it does near the beginning of Joe's appearance in the *Follies,* seems to take place in 1918. Independent evidence, however, suggests that the material immediately following that story—the incident involving Joe at Billy LaHiff's Tavern, with its mention of Damon Runyon and Bugs Baer—actually occurred sometime in 1924. LaHiff's was a hangout for show business people in the 1920s and was the site of the Friar's Club testimonial dinner for Walter Winchell in September 1924 that figures in a later Joe and Loretta anecdote.[8] Further, Damon Runyon, Bugs Baer, and Harry Richman shared an apartment over LaHiff's restaurant in 1924.

It is therefore highly probable that the LaHiff's stories and even the Houdini anecdote at the Friar's funeral occurred at least in the 1920s, if not specifically in 1924. And Lowry's mention of the popularity of Joe's jazz dance and of the many imitations of Joe, including the ones featured in a Frisco dance contest, suggests that the surrounding stories date from an even later period, the mid to late 1920s, the height of Joe's career.[9]

Lowry's placement of Joe's reunion with Loretta after these stories makes their relationship appear to have lasted much longer—and therefore to have had a much more damaging influence on Joe—than was probably the case.[10]

If Joe's reunion with Loretta actually occurred during his *Follies* engagement, as Lowry suggests, Loretta most probably returned to Joe around September or October of 1918. Joe may in fact have left the *Follies* in October 1918 in part because Ziegfeld refused to make Loretta part of Joe's act.[11]

Lowry says that Joe did not play the Palace Theatre in New York until immediately after his *Follies* run, and the *Variety* notice of Joe's "new act" on October 11, 1918, places him at the Palace.

Loretta performed in her own act the week of August 23, 1918, doing an imitation of Joe's jazz dance, complete with cigar. Both Joe and Loretta were reviewed as part of the Fifth Avenue bill on October 24, 1918, and were included in the Palace bill on November 11, 1918. Another review of Joe and Loretta was published the week of January 31, 1919. On January 9, 1920, however, Joe was listed in *Variety* as part of a new act with Pauline Chambers and three musicians. This evidence suggests that Joe and Loretta were no longer together at that time and that their reunion lasted only about twelve to eighteen months. Lowry implies two contradictory possibilities, that Joe's second break with Loretta occurred after the Friar's club incident in 1924 or after Joe's appearance in Earl Carroll's *Vanities* in 1928. The 1924 date is possible but not probable, and the 1928 date seems impossible.

With or without Loretta, Joe worked steadily after his appearance in the *Follies*. During the late teens and early twenties, he appeared as part of a duo—first with Loretta and then with Pauline Chambers. From about 1926 to 1929, Joe was listed in reviews and *Variety* playbills only as a single act, although he probably appeared with both musicians and assistants (probably female).[12] "Frisco and Co," including Loretta, appeared at the Riverside for the weeks of November 18 and 22, 1918. At the Orpheum in Brooklyn he attempted and failed to get top billing during the week of November 29, 1918. *Variety* also reports a run-in with Aileen Bronson (of the duo Laurie and Bronson) during his appearance at the Brooklyn Orpheum on December 6, 1918. Joe performed at the Bushwick in Brooklyn the week of December 9; he was engaged for a one-night stand at the Orpheum, Brooklyn, on December 22 and was at the Fifth Avenue December 23–25, 1918. "Frisco Co" appeared at Keith's Royal in Brooklyn the week of January 6, 1919.[13] Joe and Loretta appeared together at the Colonial the week of January 24, 1919, and "Frisco Co" was at Keith's Palace in New York the week of January 27 (vaudeville acts often "doubled," playing two locations during the same period). Joe played the Palace again the week of January 31 but was gone by the week of February 3; he then appeared at Keith's Alhambra in New York the week of February 10, 1919.

During this time a rather interesting event occurred that Lowry does not mention. On January 17, 1919, *Variety* reported that Joe would join the cast of Arthur Hammerstein's musical version of *Seven Days,* called *Slumber Party* (subsequently renamed *Tumble In*). But according to the January 31 issue of *Variety,* the show opened without Joe Frisco, who, after bragging that "he'd be a Broadway star in two weeks," had been dumped from the cast for appearing in vaudeville clubs instead of attending rehearsals.

After Joe became a recognized vaudeville star, Lowry reports, he toured the Orpheum Circuit and visited his mother, now in Dubuque. Given the several Orpheum performances listed above, these events probably occurred between November 18, 1918, and February 1919. But Lowry also states that during his Orpheum tour Joe visited a Los Angeles movie set and "watched Rudolph Valentino break the heart of Natasha Rambova while three tired musicians created the mood by playing 'Hearts and Flowers.'" However, Rambova, Valentino's wife, set designer, and producer, never appeared in a film with Valentino. Her only film was *When Love Grows Cold,* released in 1926, after she was separated from Valentino. Furthermore, Joe probably would not have seen either Rambova or Valentino, even separately, until after both were well known, so this event probably occurred no earlier than the release of Valentino's film *The Sheik* in 1922, and more likely after the 1924 release of *Monsieur Beaucaire,* a film that Rambova wrote and directed for Valentino. Also, the performance dates listed above leave rather little time for a trip to the West Coast. Either Lowry invented this visit to Hollywood, or the text contains another chronological jump in addition to the confusion about dramatis personae.

After this point in Lowry's account, most of the verifiable incidents he reports can be located fairly firmly in the mid to late 1920s. In fact, the next major event in Joe's career that we can identify, an event that Lowry places just after Joe's return from his Orpheum circuit tour in 1918–1919, was his signing contracts to appear with W. C. Fields in Earl Carroll's *Vanities,* produced in 1928. The exchanges between Fields and Joe probably took place between June and August 1928. This edition of the *Vanities* opened at the Earl Carroll Theatre in New York on August 8, 1928, and gave two hundred performances.[14]

Lowry next tells us that after the close of the *Vanities*—that is, probably sometime in 1929—Joe and Loretta resumed their act at the Palace, and that Walter Winchell panned Loretta's performance. Not only is it highly unlikely that Joe and Loretta were still together in 1929, but the Friar's Club testimonial dinner for Winchell that (according to Lowry) Joe said he could not attend for fear of losing Loretta occurred on September 14, 1924, the day before Winchell left his job with the *Vaudeville News* to take a position with the *Graphic*.[15] Again, the romance narrative device has invaded and distorted the general chronology.[16]

Furthermore, Lowry associates what he calls Joe's "momma complex" with the romance narrative. In Lowry's story, Joe's decision to begin building a house for his mother seems to occur during one of his first engagements at the Palace. And several pages after Lowry's account of the Winchell dinner, with its misleading emphasis on Loretta, we are told that Joe's mother's house is "progressing nicely."

Between these two points, Lowry reports, Joe has not only hired an architect to begin work on his mother's house, but also visited his mother and returned to Chicago. Then, during the "dwindling days of the roaring twenties" when vaudeville was "fading," he travels to Los Angeles and visits movie studios with Bryan Foy, who has produced *Lights of New York*, a film that was, Lowry states, "the first all-talking movie."[17] The appearance of *Lights* in 1928 is one of the few firm anchors in a sea of chronological probabilities. The chances are good that Joe actually initiated the work on his mother's house after 1928, not in either 1919 or 1924. Despite his inveterate gambling, Joe would by this time have commanded a high enough salary to afford such a project.

Immediately after the events surrounding the building of Mrs. Joseph's house, Lowry returns to the Joe and Loretta theme and tells the story of their second breakup and the "reunion" of the married Loretta and Eddie Cox with Joe in Philadelphia. As we have noted, Joe's relationship with Loretta was probably over by January 1920. Why, then, has Lowry interwoven it throughout his account of Joe's career during the 1920s?

One is inclined here to suspect the influence of the tragic clown archetype. Joe was obviously at the height of his career in the late 1920s, drawing both critical praise and high salaries. For example, he played the Palace in mid-January 1927 for a salary of $1,250 per engagement but was asking $1,500 per "showing." Both the *New York Times* and the *Variety* obituaries report that "at one time" he pulled down as much as fifty thousand dollars a year. By emphasizing Joe's "momma complex" and his unrequited love for Loretta, Lowry establishes a dramatic tension between Joe's outward success and his inner pain, as well as an emotional justification for Joe's errant ways.

The chapter entitled "This Gorilla Was a Killer" begins a succession of anecdotes about events that we can be fairly sure occurred in the 1930s and 1940s. Joe appeared in Bryan Foy's version of *The Gorilla* in the role of Garrity, a blundering detective. Although Lowry states that this film is "still in the can on the shelf," it was released in 1931.

Lowry also reports Joe's statement that this film would be his "first" and his "last," but in reality Joe appeared in seven other films between 1938 and 1957: *Western Jamboree* (1938), *Ride, Tenderfoot, Ride* (1940), *Atlantic City* (1944), *Shady Lady* (1945), *That's My Man* (1947), *Riding High* (1950), and *The Sweet Smell of Success* (1957). Most of these films were probably used as "vaudfilms," material that increasingly replaced live acts in vaudeville theaters in the 1930s and 1940s. *The Sweet Smell of Success,* however, is a critically acclaimed example of the "film noir" genre. Joe's film credits therefore include eight motion pictures, although Lowry mentions only *The Gorilla* and *Atlantic City.*

The start of the chapter "This Gorilla Was a Killer" briefly continues the chronologically dislocated account of Joe, Loretta, and Eddie Cox but then moves into Joe's experiences in Los Angeles, Hollywood, and Beverly Hills. Lowry also implies that Joe's mother's house was completed in 1930, during the filming of *The Gorilla.* The house was apparently begun and finished between 1928 and 1930—a fairly long incubation, but the fact that Joe had to take care of "back payments, fines, and liens" suggests that the completion of the house was delayed by Joe's somewhat inconsistent financial support of the project.

Joe's visit to his senile mother in the newly completed house probably occurred in or near 1930. His subsequent escapes to Chicago and to Florida are impossible to document precisely, but Joe probably made numerous trips to the Midwest and the South, both on and off the vaudeville circuits. Lowry's account conflates them into one or two episodes as venues for his Frisco anecdotes.

We have clear evidence from *Variety* that Joe appeared, at least on film,

AN ESSAY ON CHRONOLOGY 143

in the New York area fairly steadily throughout the 1930s. For example, he performed at Loew's State in New York City the weeks of January 2 and January 9, 1930. The week of February 1–5, 1930, he apparently appeared in "vaudfilm" both at Loew's State and across the street at the Astor.[18] From a *Variety* story about Amos and Andy at the Palace dated January 22, 1930, we know that Joe himself was in New York—and probably performing—during this period. Halfway through this decade Joe was still appearing—live, apparently—in New York City at Jim Healey's from September 27, 1935, to February 21, 1936, a long run that places him fairly securely in the New York area.

At some point between 1931 and 1937, however, Joe permanently relocated in the Los Angeles and Palm Springs area.[19] The chronology now moves into the late 1930s, 1940s, and early 1950s, the last days of vaudeville. Lowry's first mention of Joe's troubles with the IRS, an episode possibly belonging with the stories about much later tax problems, makes the point that Joe's popularity had fallen off drastically—he now made only five hundred dollars a week.

Near the start of this period Joe began performing at Charlie Foy's supper club in the San Fernando Valley. It is difficult to date this event with any precision because Joe worked for Foy only informally (Lowry states that Joe refused to go on Foy's payroll because of his tax difficulties). There are, however, references in the text and evidence from *Variety* that give us approximate dates for this period. First, Joe and Charlie Foy appeared together at the Grace Hayes Lodge in the Los Angeles area from February 24, 1939, to October 27, 1939.[20] This fact suggests either that the Foy Supper Club did not yet exist or that it was new and not yet financially self-supporting.[21]

Second, Lowry reports that the incident involving Joe and Bette Davis occurred on the evening that she was awarded an Oscar for best actress. Bette Davis garnered awards for best actress in 1936 for *Dangerous* and in 1939 for *Jezebel*. Since Joe worked steadily in New York in 1936, the later date fits more reasonably into the general chronology.

Finally, at a testimonial dinner for Joe at the Masquers Club near the end of his life, Joe stated that he had worked for Foy for fifteen years. Because the testimonial dinner anecdote concerns the salary that Charlie paid Joe, we can infer that the "fifteen years" refers to the period after Joe agreed to accept payment for his performances—probably from the early 1940s to a time near his death in 1958. This chronology also squares nicely with Lowry's report of Joe's last years. Other evidence, such as Joe's joining the cast of *Atlantic City* in 1943, also suggests that Joe stayed near Foy's supper club during the closing decades of his career.

Within the general chronology of Joe's activities during the 1940s and 1950s, Loretta McDermott, whose role as Joe's nemesis has now been partly taken over by the IRS, distorts the picture. Immediately after the account of Joe's appearance in *Atlantic City* (1944), Lowry skips forward to Joe's frequent appearances on Tom Duggan's television show, whose popularity was at its height during the late 1950s.[22] Lowry then immediately introduces Loretta's reappearance in the form of a long-distance call to Joe from Cleveland, a juxtaposition which suggests that Loretta's call occurred during the 1950s.

Lowry, however, also reports that this call arrived at almost the precise moment when Joe was offered a part in *Atlantic City* and that Joe managed to finish his performance in the film before "Rasputin" located Loretta employed as a hatcheck "girl" in Chicago at the Grant Hotel, the same place where she had performed (no doubt without Joe) "a quarter of a century before." It makes sense within the framework of the general chronology to date Loretta's Grant Hotel performance in the 1920s and her call in the 1950s, but in that case the call could not have come during Joe's work on *Atlantic City*. There is no evidence in Lowry's account or outside it that Joe actually found Loretta, either in 1943 or in the 1950s. But even her minimal appearance here in Lowry's narrative causes him to conflate dates for events occurring in the mid-1950s and in 1943. By this point it has become evident that Lowry has been at some pains throughout his account to present Loretta as an inveterate loser—not only a two-timer and possibly the onetime wife of a gangster, but also a failure and a drunk. How accurate this picture of Loretta is, we cannot know, but there is some evidence that it is exaggerated.[23] Lowry seems to recast characters in the same way that he reforms chronology in his attempt to lend unity to Joe's life.

Another problematic conjunction is the one that contends that just as Joe finishes up his film performance, and during the discussion between

Charlie Foy and Joe about Rasputin's discovery of Loretta at the Grant, the Internal Revenue Service again calls Joe on the carpet. Foy reportedly tells the IRS investigator that Joe is "over sixty." But Joe could not have been over sixty in 1943.

The most likely direction in which we might adjust Lowry's account is to assume that Loretta resurfaced, not in 1943, but in the 1950s and that the film from which the IRS garnisheed Joe's wages was not *Atlantic City,* but either *Riding High,* a Bing Crosby film that appeared in 1950, or *The Sweet Smell of Success,* which appeared in 1957. Either date would reconcile the tax stories with the Tom Duggan anecdotes from the 1950s.

Although the whole story of Foy's intercession with the IRS on Joe's behalf could be wrong, it is also likely that both the earlier story about Joe's tax problems and this later one conflate incidents to represent ongoing problems that Joe encountered with the IRS throughout his career. In any case, Joe's appearance in *Atlantic City,* Loretta's reappearance, and Joe's starring role in an Internal Revenue Service investigation cannot all have occurred exactly as Lowry tells them during "a full week of heartaches"— either in 1943 or in the 1950s. The juxtaposition of Loretta McDermott with the IRS probably reflects Lowry's unconscious attempt to create a dramatic climax for Joe's life, one that will bring both of the two major villains— Loretta and the IRS—on stage at once.

One other piece of evidence suggests a relatively late date for Joe's tax problems. At the beginning of Lowry's chapter "Pass the 'Milltowns,' Please," he again mentions Joe's "week of heartaches" and then tells us that immediately afterward Joe was invited to appear with Bing Crosby in a picture that Crosby was making for David Butler. Although Lowry does not name this film, *Riding High,* released in 1950, is the only film in which Bing Crosby and Joe Frisco both appear.[24] This fact further indicates that the events of this chapter and most of the stories in the preceding one, except for those that mention Loretta, belong to the late 1940s and 1950s.

As Lowry's account suggests, Joe's last illness was relatively short. The *New York Times* reports that Joe "had been ill for several months" before his death. His last residence was the Motion Picture Country House and Hospital in Woodland Hills, California. *Variety* mentions several testimonial dinners for Joe shortly before his death; the dinner at the Masquers Club that Lowry presents in detail is probably the one held in January 1958 and mentioned in Joe's *New York Times* obituary.[25] A performer to the end, Joe also appeared on a radio show in mid-January, four weeks before he died. And the *New York Times* reports that "[a] few days before his death, Frisco was voted an honorary membership by the American Guild of Variety Artists." Although the *New York Times* and *Variety* obituaries give Joe's age at his death as sixty-eight, he was probably nearer sixty-five years old. Joe Frisco, dancer, comedian, and consummate clown, died of cancer on February 16, 1958.

Notes

1. The chronology reconstructed in this essay was gathered from three areas: (1) primary sources like *Variety*, the N*ew York Times,* and the *Chicago Tribune;* (2) histories, dictionaries, and encyclopedias of vaudeville, theater, and film; and (3) biographies and autobiographies of celebrities, for example, Bill Robinson, Walter Winchell, and Damon Runyon.

2. I am here indebted to Nancy Mann for her observations about Lowry's narrational motivations. Lowry's fear that readers may see Foy and Frisco as homosexual is evident in his chapter "The Joker Is Wild," in which he says, "The relationship between Foy and Frisco was beautiful. They had great affection for one another, in spite of the fact that neither of the two guys sang soprano."

3. *Over the River* opened at the Globe in New York on January 8, 1912, and played 120 performances. After this run it was no doubt taken on the road. See Walter Rigdon, *The Biographical Encyclopedia: Who's Who in American Theatre* (New York: James H. Heineman, 1965), 37.

4. Jim Haskins and N. R. Mitgang, *Mr. Bojangles: The Biography of Bill Robinson* (New York: William Morrow, 1988).

5. The evidence in *Variety* suggests that Joe performed with this group after his departure for New York in 1917 and supposedly after his breakup with Loretta. There is no suggestion that Joe worked with this group in Chicago in 1917. This discrepancy is the first of many that cast doubt on Lowry's account of the Joe and Loretta "romance" chronology.

6. *Variety,* September 5, 1927.

7. Evidence for these dates appears in a *Variety* item on August 25, 1918; but a revue called the *Midnight Frolic* was still playing at the Roof on September 27 and

was possibly scheduled to be sent out as a "road attraction" on November 1. This show reportedly played the Roof during the summer months. It is not clear, however, whether this show is different from the *Follies*.

8. Tom Clark, *The World of Damon Runyon* (New York: Harper and Row, 1978), 143–44.

9. Although there is no doubt that Joe enjoyed a significant, if fairly brief, success and that he was a major influence on his fellow performers, I strongly suspect that by the late 1920s the incursions of cinema began to erode his reputation with audiences, as it did with vaudeville itself.

10. If the ring with a diamond "as big as a grape" that Lowry says Joe gave Loretta after they were reunited indicates that they were formally engaged, there is no documented evidence of it. In fact, the *New York Times* (February 4, 1926) reports that vaudevillian "Louis Joseph" was engaged to marry an "heiress," Miss Marie Carlestos, the daughter of a "wealthy Brazilian Coffee planter," on February 7, 1926. The marriage apparently did not take place, and Lowry does not seem to be aware either of Miss Carlestos or of the engagement.

11. This meeting with Ziegfeld may have occurred around the close of the New Amsterdam Roof run, about mid-October. Despite Lowry's account, Joe could have opened at the Palace while he was still with the *Follies*.

12. The *Variety* obituary (*Variety Obituaries, 1957–63*, vol. 5 [New York: Garland, 1988]) reports that Joe "at one time" worked as "a comedy and dance twin billed as 'Frisco with McDermott & Cox.'" This item seems to be the only independent verification of Joe's collaboration with both Loretta and Cox; but the same notice reports that Joe's act was also known at one time as "Frisco & Co," a listing that in fact occurs regularly in the *Variety* playbills.

13. The "Frisco Five," now known as Bert Kelly's Jazz Band, also opened at the Tokio Supper Club the week of January 17, 1918, but Joe does not seem to have been with them.

14. Samuel L. Leiter, *The Encyclopedia of the New York Stage, 1920–1930* (Westport, Conn.: Greenwood Press, 1985), 231.

15. Walter Winchell, *Winchell Exclusive* (New York: Prentice Hall, 1975), 41, 53. Winchell wrote a column for the *News* from around 1919 to 1924.

16. If there was any other testimonial dinner at the Friars Club for Winchell, his autobiography does not mention it. Such a dinner would doubtless have occurred at a later date when he was a greater celebrity, not before 1924, when he was less well known. I cannot reconcile Joe's appearance in the *Vanities,* the anecdote about the Winchell dinner, and the probable dates of Joe's relationship with Loretta.

17. *The Jazz Singer,* the so-called first "talking film," appeared in 1927.

18. It is not clear from the *Variety* announcements whether Joe also appeared live at Loew's State during the week of January 22 as well as on film, but this is a possibility.

19. Although Lowry presents Joe's return to California and his visit to the Lone Palm as one event, the passage probably represents the entire process of Joe's permanent resettlement in the Los Angeles area. Assuming that the events that involve Bert Wheeler, Harry Akst, and others occurred when Wheeler and Woolsey were a comedy team in the movies, the date here is definitely after 1929; however, Anthony Slide's *The Encyclopedia of Vaudeville* (1994) dates the pair's first team effort as occurring in 1926. (They broke up in 1937.) The three Ritz Brothers made movies together after 1934; Al Jolson appeared in films from 1927 (*The Jazz Singer*) on, and Harry Akst appeared in the movies between 1929 and 1933. Joe Laurie's *Vaudeville* (1953), however, states that Akst accompanied Al Jolson "on all his tours," and this fact perhaps confirms a late date for these events. Jimmy Durante started in pictures in 1930. If we boldly assume that all these entertainers were in California to make movies, these events took place sometime between 1930 and 1937.

20. All references to Joe in the New York area playbills in *Variety* disappear at this point also.

21. Lowry's observation that Joe's "popularity" at Foy's club "brought in enough money for the club to prosper" also suggests that Joe probably began to perform at the club when it was fairly new.

22. This information is found in Duggan's *Variety* obituary notice dated June 4, 1969.

23. At one time she was apparently doing well enough to "perform" for six weeks at a club "which bore her name," the Loretta McDermott on West Fifty-second Street in New York. The April 16, 1929, *New York Times* reports that Loretta was fined $150 and given a year's probation for breaking the liquor laws. Loretta pleaded guilty and the judge commended her for her "honest" plea and, presumably, for the fact that she would not swear that she "did not know liquor when she saw it," as did at least one other defendant. The *Times* also reports rather inscrutably that Loretta's lawyer insisted that "his client's six weeks employment at the Loretta McDermott Club was her 'first and last venture' of this kind" and that she was "unpaid for her services."

24. This film is not listed in David Butler's film credits, but it may have been either a "vaudfilm" or a minor entry in a similar genre.

25. *New York Times,* Tuesday, February 18, 1958, 27.

Selected Bibliography

Adams, Joey. 1968. "Happiness Was a Thing Called F-F-Frisco." *Coronet,* April, 50–54.
Bordman, Gerald. 1984. *The Oxford Companion to American Theatre.* New York: Oxford University Press.
Breslin, Jimmy. 1991. *Damon Runyon.* New York: Ticknor & Fields.
Bronner, Edwin. 1980. *The Encyclopedia of the American Theatre, 1900–1975.* New York: A. S. Barnes.
Brunn, H. O. 1960. *The Story of the Original Dixieland Jazz Band.* Baton Rouge: Louisiana State University Press. [See pp. 26–27.]
Clark, Tom. 1978. *The World of Damon Runyon.* New York: Harper & Row.
DiMeglio, John E. 1973. *Vaudeville U.S.A.* Bowling Green, Ohio: Bowling Green University Popular Press.
Erenberg, Lewis A. 1981. *Steppin' Out: New York Nightlife and the Transformation of American Culture, 1890–1930.* Westport, Conn.: Greenwood Press.
Gilbert, Douglas. 1940. *American Vaudeville: Its Life and Times.* New York: Whittlesey House.
Green, Abel, ed. 1952. *The Spice of Variety.* New York: Henry Holt.
Green, Abel, and Joe Laurie, Jr. 1951. *Show Biz from Vaude to Video.* New York: Henry Holt.
Halliwell, Leslie. 1977. *The Filmgoer's Companion,* 6th ed. New York: Avon.
Haskins, Jim, and N. R. Mitgang. 1988. *Mr. Bojangles: The Biography of Bill Robinson.* New York: William Morrow.
Hayes, Peter Lind. 1967. "A Character Called Frisco." *Variety,* January 4, 34.
———. 1951. "M-M-M-Meet J-J-J-Joe F-F-F-Frisco." *Collier's,* December 1, 20–21, 50, 52.
Henderson, Mary C. 1973. *The City and the Theatre: New York Playhouses from Bowling Green to Times Square.* Clifton, N.J.: James T. White.
Holbrook, Dick. 1976. "Mister Jazz Himself—The Story of Ray Lopez." *Storyville,* no. 64 (April–May), 135–51. [See p. 138.]

Irwin, Ben. 1981. "Joe Frisco: He Stuttered to the Top." *Los Angeles Times,* Calendar section, April 19, 4.
Jacobs, Lewis. 1967. *The Rise of the American Film: A Critical History.* New York: Teachers College Press, Columbia University, 1967.
La Beau, Dennis, ed. 1979. *Theatre, Film, and Television Biographies Master Index.* Detroit: Gale Research.
Langman, Larry. 1987. *Encyclopedia of American Film Comedy.* New York: Garland.
Laurie, Joe, Jr. 1953. *Vaudeville: From the Honky-Tonks to the Palace.* New York: Henry Holt.
Leiter, Samuel L. 1985. *The Encyclopedia of the New York Stage, 1920–1930.* Westport, Conn.: Greenwood Press.
Nadel, Ira B. 1993. "Biography and Theory, or Beckett in the Bath." In *Biography and Autobiography: Essays on Irish and Canadian History and Literature,* ed. James Noonan. Ottawa: Carleton University Press. [See pp. 9–17.]
Nash, Jay Robert, and Ralph Ross Stanley. 1987. *The Motion Picture Guide Index.* Chicago: Cinebooks.
Nowlan, Robert A., and Gwendolyn Wright Nowlan. 1989. *Cinema Sequels and Remakes: 1903–1987.* Jefferson, N.C.: McFarland.
Rigdon, Walter. 1965. *The Biographical Encyclopaedia and Who's Who of the American Theatre.* New York: James H. Heineman.
Sklar, Robert. 1977. *Movie-Made America: A Cultural History of American Movies.* New York: Vintage Books.
Slide, Anthony. 1944. *The Encyclopedia of Vaudeville.* Westport, Conn.: Greenwood Press.
———. 1981. *The Vaudevillians: A Dictionary of Vaudeville Performers.* Westport, Conn.: Arlington House.
Snyder, Robert W. 1989. *The Voice of the City: Vaudeville and Popular Culture in New York.* New York: Oxford University Press.
Syme, Sir Ronald. 1971. "Bad Trip." In *New York Review of Books.* January 7, 40.
Taylor, Robert. 1989. *Fred Allen: His Life and Wit.* Boston: Little, Brown.
Thomas, Nicholas, ed. 1990. *International Dictionary of Films and Filmmakers.* Vol. 1. Chicago: Saint James Press.
Wertheim, Arthur Frank. 1983. "The Rise and Fall of Milton Berle." In *American History, American Television: Interpreting the Video Past,* ed. John E. O'Connor. New York: Frederick Ungar. [See pp. 55–78.]
Wilson, Earl. 1949. "The 'Rapier Retort.'" In *Let 'Em Eat Cheesecake.* Garden City, N.Y.: Doubleday. [See pp. 44–48.]
Winchell, Walter. 1975. *Winchell Exclusive: "Things That Happened to Me—and Me to Them."* Englewood Cliffs, N.J.: Prentice-Hall.

Index

Academy Awards, 74
Akst, Harry, 97
Albee, E. F., 52
Allen, Fred, 15, 135. *See also* James, Freddie
American Hospital, 35
"Am I Blue" (Clarke), 6
Amsterdam, Morey, 104
Andrews, Lois, 8
Armed Forces special services film unit, xviii
Astaire, Fred, 9
Atlantic City (1944), 142, 144
Atlantic City (N. J.), 54
Autry, Gene, 87, 102

Baer, Bugs, 47–48, 138
Bayes, Nora, xix
Bay View (horse), 80–81
Belmont Park Racetrack, 4
Benny, Jack, 102
Bent, Marion, 50
Berle, Milton, xxii
Berlin, Irving, 5
Bijou Dream (theatre), 24
Billy LaHiff's Tavern, 47, 138
Bojangles. *See* Robinson, Bill
Brice, Fanny, 5
Bronson, Aileen, 139
Brooks, Shelton, 45
Brown, Harry Joe, 101–2
Brown Derby (restaurant), 10
Buchanon, Irving Agency, 18
Buck, Gene, 3, 6
Busher (horse), 9
"buskers," 12

Butler, David, 95–96, 145
Butterfield Circuit, 136
Buttram, Pat, 102, 103, 104, 105

Carlestos, Marie, 147n. 10
Carroll Theatre, 54
Casimir Theatre, 24
Catlett, Walter, 3
"Celebrities" (stage show), xix–xx
Chambers, Pauline, 139
Charney, King, 67, 68
Chasen, Dave, 9–10, 54–55
Chi-Chi Club, 66, 67, 68, 69
Chocolate Nijinsky. *See* Robinson, Bill
Choen, Carl, 66, 68
Clark, Andy, 19, 21, 28, 34–35
Clarke, Grant, 5, 6, 41
Club 18, 66
Cohen, Myron, 101
Colonial Theatre, 45, 48
Cook, Joe, 54
Cooper, George W., 136
Costello, Lou, 66–67, 68
Cox, Eddie, 57, 58, 59–60, 89, 147n. 12
Crosby, Bing, 10–11, 71, 86, 95–96, 97, 145
Curtis, Jack, 52, 55

"Darktown Strutters' Ball, The" (Brooks), 4, 45, 49, 91, 96
Darling, Eddie, 52
Davies, Marion, 5
Davis, Bette, 74, 143
Davis Theatre, 53–54
DeLacey, Kitty, 16, 17
Del Mar Racetrack, 64

Dempsey, Jack, 103–4
Dixieland Five, 20–21, 22, 27, 28, 33, 136, 146n. 5
"Dr. Kronkhite" (comedy routine), 45
Duggan, Tom, 89, 144, 145
"dumps," 24
Durante, Jimmy, 68

Eddie Foy and the Seven Little Foys, xviii, 50, 54
Edwards, Cliff, 52, 104
Edwards, Gus, xviii, 8, 16, 42, 135–36
Edwards, Hank, 28, 32

Fay, Frank, 46–47, 95
Feinberg, Nate, 1–2
Fields, W. C., 55, 140
Fitzgerald, F. Scott, xvii
Fitzgerald, Harry, 3, 38–41, 51–52
Follies (stage show), 137–39. *See also* Ziegfeld, Florenz
Ford, Wally, 105
Foy, Bryan (Brynie), 58, 61, 62–64, 141
Foy, Charlie, xvii–xviii, 10–11, 58, 103; acts, 71, 73–74; cat incident, 71–73; death of Frisco's mother and, 84–85; Duggan's show and, 89; film credits, xviii; friendship with Frisco, 54, 85, 88, 135; IRS and, 92–94, 145; "Max" incident, 74–77; McDermott and, 89–90; at racetrack, 77–82; supper club, xvii–xviii, 70, 87–88, 143–44; turkey incident, 88
Foy, Eddie, xviii, 12, 50, 54, 135
Foy, Eddie, Sr., 52
Foy, Mary, 73
Friars Club, 46–47, 48, 52, 55–56, 138, 147n. 16
Frisco, Joe: in Battle Creek, 24–25; Broadway debut, 4–5, 38–39, 46; in Chicago, 14–19; childhood, 12; depression, 42–43, 57, 134; film appearances, 142–43; illiteracy, 7, 14, 15, 62; illness, 97, 98–99, 100, 145; imitators, 8–9; IRS and, 69, 92–94, 143, 145; as jazz dancer, xvii, 4–5, 25, 33–34, 136; in Los Angeles, 66–67, 148n. 19; as master of ceremonies, xix; in Miami, 39–41, 66; at Motion Picture Country Home, 100–101, 145; New Orleans tour, 19–23; in New York, 46–55, 66, 142–43; in Palm Springs, 66–69; racetrack betting, 9, 44–45, 61, 63–64, 66, 68, 77–79, 85–86, 97–98, 98, 134; road tours, 53–54; salaries, 39, 52, 87, 96, 141–42; stutter, 3–4; television appearances, 89, 144; Ziegfeld and, 3–4, 51
Fritzel, Mike, 28, 33, 136, 137
Frolics Cafe, 57

Generaux, Fenn, 56–57
Glaser, Joe, 87
Globe (theatre), 137
Gorilla, The (1931), 61–64, 137, 142
Grant, Cary, 9
Grauman, Sid, 83
Grauman's Chinese Theatre, 83
Great Gatsby, The (Fitzgerald), xvii
Great Northern Hippodrome (theatre), 14–15, 135
Green Mill Gardens (night club), 41, 42

Hal Roach Studio, xviii
Hammerstein, Arthur, 140
Handman, Lou, xx
Hanlon, Bert, 63
Hearst, William Randolph, 5
"Heart Aches and Horse Laffs" (Lowry and Foy), xxi
Hippodrome (theatre), 14–15, 135
Hodkins Booking Agency, 21
Hollywood Park Racetrack, 77–79
"Horse Room, The" (comedy routine), 79–80, 91
Hurley, Connie, 81

"If I Had My Life to Live Over (song)," 104
Inter-Ocean Hotel, 24
Irving, Mr., 18

James, Freddie, 14–15
jazz dance, xvii, 4–5, 25, 33–34, 136
Jessel, George, 8, 58–59

INDEX

Jiminy Cricket, 52
Joe Frisco and the Dixieland Five, 28
"Joe Frisco Night," 101–5
John's Rendezvous (restaurant), 95–96
Jolson, Al, 67, 68, 97–98, 104–5
Joseph, Charles, 28, 31–32, 35, 136
Joseph, Louis Wilson. *See* Frisco, Joe
Joseph, Mae, 30, 36, 57, 65–66, 84
Joseph, Momma, 28–30, 35, 56–57, 65–66, 84; Lowry's chronology and, 134, 141, 142
Joseph, Poppa, 13, 28–30, 31–32, 50, 136–37

Katleman, Jake, 68
Kedzie Theatre, 28
Keith, B. F., 48
Kirk, Joe, 101, 103

Las Vegas (Nev.), 68
La Vere, Florrie. *See* Lowry, Florrie
Lehr, Lew, 19
Let 'Em Eat Cheesecake (1949), xvii
Lewis, Joe E., 41
Lichtman, Al, 79
Lichtman, Rose, 79
Lights of New York (1928), 58, 141
Lone Palm (motel), 66–67, 148n. 19
Loretta McDermott Club, 148n. 23
Louisiana Lo-Downs, 39
Lowry, Ed, xvii, xviii, 133–34
Lowry, Florrie, xix–xx
Lyman, Abe, 56

Mack, Roy, 41, 42, 43
Majestic Theatre, 14, 56, 57, 135
"Man in the Horse Room" (comedy routine), 79–80, 89
Martin, Robert, xxii
Marx, Chico, 9
Masquers Club, 101, 143–44, 145–46
Max (gambler), 74–75, 77
Mayer, Louis B., 9
McCarthy, Neil S., 9
McDermott, Loretta, 16, 36, 48–51; Cox and, 59–60, 89, 141, 147n. 12; as drinker, 91, 94, 144, 148n. 23; Grant Hotel incident, 89–92, 94, 144–45; Gus Edwards and, 8, 17, 135–36; Hank Edwards and, 28, 32, 34, 37–38; Lowry's chronology and, 134, 135–36, 140–41, 144–45; New Orleans tour, 19–23; Ziegfeld and, 51, 138–39
Meakin, Walter, 24, 27
Midnight Frolic (stage show), 41, 44, 146–47n. 7
Mike Fritzel's Cafe, 28, 33–34, 136, 137
Mills, Evelyn Florence. *See* Lowry, Florrie
monkey episode, 18–19
Moranda, Madeline, xviii
Mosconi, Lou, 48
"My Sweetie Went Away (song)," 18

Nadel, Ira, xxii
Nemo Theatre, 21
New Amsterdam Roof (theatre), 41, 137–38, 146–47n. 7
Nick the Greek, 79
Norworth, Jack, 45

"Oh How I Laugh When I Think How I Cried over You" (song), 60
Orpheum Circuit, 14, 54, 140
Over the River (play), 12, 50, 135

Palace Theatre, xx, 18, 50, 52–53, 56, 136, 139, 140–41
Palladium (London), xix
Palm Springs (Calif.), 66–68
Parkyakarkus, 46
Pepper, Jack, 66, 67, 69, 104, 105
Perino's (restaurant), 10
Pink Poodle (tavern), 19, 20
Portnoy, Frank, 68
Prince, Irene "Teddy," xviii, xix, xx

Rabwin, Marcus, 100
Raft, George, 78
Rambova, Natasha, 54, 140
Rasputin, 42, 48–49, 57, 91–92, 94
Rector's (tavern), 39
Rendezvous (restaurant), 39
Republic Pictures, 88–89, 91
Rhodes, Billy, 48

Richards, Cully, 73, 87, 102–3
Richman, Harry, 5–6, 138
Ride, Tenderfoot, Ride (1940), 142
Riding High (1950), 145
Ritz, Al, 9, 68, 78–79
Ritz, Harry, 67, 68
Ritz Brothers, 67, 68, 148n. 19
Roberts, Benny, 53
Robinson, Bill (Bojangles), 24–27, 33–34, 136
Rogers, Will, 5
Roof Garden. *See* New Amsterdam Roof
Rooney, Pat, 50
Rooney, Pat, Jr., 93
Rosenbloom, Maxie, 79
Rothstein, Bill, 39, 40
Runyon, Damon, 47–48, 138

Sans Souci (restaurant), 17–18
Santa Anita Racetrack, 9, 97–98
Schindler's (theatre), 18
School Days (play), xviii, 8
Seven Little Foys, The (1955), xviii
Shady Lady (1945), 142
Sherman House (hotel), 66
Shore, Sylvia, 40
Silverman, Sime, 53
Skouras brothers, xix
Smith, Bill, 67
Smith and Dale, 45
"Some of These Days (Brooks)," 45
Starr, Jimmy, 61
Strand Theatre, 25
suitcase actors, 24
Sweet Sixteen Bathing Beauties, 43
Sweet Smell of Success, The (1957), 142, 145
Syme, Ronald, xxii

"Take Me Out to the Ball Game" (Norworth), 45
Tanguay, Eva, 35
Tannen, Julius, 104
television, xxi–xxii
Texaco Star Theatre, xxii
That's My Man (1947), 142
Thorek, Max, 35–36
Tibbett, Lawrence, 71
tragic clown archetype, 141–42

Ukelele Ike. *See* Edwards, Cliff
Unique Theatre, 24
United Services Organization (USO) Camp Shows, xix

Valentino, Rudolph, 54, 140
Van Buren, Grace, 24
Vanities (1928), 54–55, 139, 140
Variety, xvii, 53, 136, 137, 138, 139, 142–43, 146
vaudeville, xx, xxi–xxii, 57–58
vaudfilms, 141–42
Verdi Theatre, 18
Victoria Theatre, 18
Vitaphone shorts, xviii

Wall, Nick, 64, 80–81
Warner Brothers, xviii, 58
Wertheim, Arthur Frank, xxi–xxii
Western Jamboree (1938), 142
Westrope, Jackie, 80
Wheeler, Bert, 67
Whiting, Margaret, 73
Wilson, Earl, xvii
Winchell, Walter, xvii, 6–7, 104–5, 141, 147n. 16; on McDermott, 55–56
Wright, Jim, 103

Ziegfeld, Florenz, 3–4, 41, 51, 137, 138–39

PAUL M. LEVITT, a professor of English at the University of Colorado at Boulder, teaches modern drama and theatre history. He is the author of books on medicine, tales for children, radio plays for the BBC, and a vaudeville about Harry Houdini, as well as books and articles on theatre.